LONDON

S Laurens Poultrey

FLUVIU

THE BRITISH LIBRARY

DIARY
2006

HISTORIC
CITY MAPS

FRANCES LINCOLN

Frances Lincoln Limited
4 Torriano Mews
Torriano Avenue
London NW5 2RZ
www.franceslincoln.com

The British Library Diary 2006
Published in association with The British Library, London
Copyright © Frances Lincoln Limited 2005
Illustrations copyright © The British Library Board 2005

All images in this diary are taken from a British Library/
University of California Press publication *Cities of the World:
A History in Maps* by Peter Whitfield

Astronomical information reproduced, with permission,
from data supplied by HM Nautical Almanac Office, copyright
© Council for the Central Laboratory of the Research Councils.

British Library cataloguing-in-publication data
A catalogue record for this book is available from
The British Library

ISBN 0-7112-2510-9
Printed in China

First Frances Lincoln edition 2005

FRONT COVER
Cambridge, drawn in 1547 by Richard Lyne. The layout of the
inner city is unchanged, but most of the colleges have been
rebuilt on classical lines. Maps C.24.a.27

BACK COVER
Palmanova, the archetypal planned, symmetrical city of the
Renaissance, built by the Venetians as a defensive fortress
against the Austrians, and completed in 1603. Maps C.29.e.1

ENDPAPERS
London, part of the Visscher panorama of 1616. Old St Paul's is
seen across the river, and the Globe Theatre is in the
foreground. Maps 162.o.1

TITLE PAGE
Details from a map of Tangier c.1675, by John Seller. Maps 7.
Tab.77 (19)

IMPRINT PAGE
Mesopotamia, the birthplace of the city and also the source of
the earliest series of city images. The Assyrian king, Sennacherib,
sits enthroned within the walls of Nineveh. Cup 648.c.1, pl.77

OVERLEAF
Beijing, a woodcut map c.1900 showing the strict,
chequerboard layout of the ancient city, which still survives; to
the south stands the outer city, built in the sixteenth-century
Ming period. Maps 30.b.54

CALENDAR 2006

JANUARY
M	T	W	T	F	S	S
						1
2	3	4	5	6	7	8
9	10	11	12	13	14	15
16	17	18	19	20	21	22
23	24	25	26	27	28	29
30	31					

FEBRUARY
M	T	W	T	F	S	S
	1	2	3	4	5	
6	7	8	9	10	11	12
13	14	15	16	17	18	19
20	21	22	23	24	25	26
27	28					

MARCH
M	T	W	T	F	S	S
	1	2	3	4	5	
6	7	8	9	10	11	12
13	14	15	16	17	18	19
20	21	22	23	24	25	26
27	28	29	30	31		

APRIL
M	T	W	T	F	S	S
					1	2
3	4	5	6	7	8	9
10	11	12	13	14	15	16
17	18	19	20	21	22	23
24	25	26	27	28	29	30

MAY
M	T	W	T	F	S	S
1	2	3	4	5	6	7
8	9	10	11	12	13	14
15	16	17	18	19	20	21
22	23	24	25	26	27	28
29	30	31				

JUNE
M	T	W	T	F	S	S
			1	2	3	4
5	6	7	8	9	10	11
12	13	14	15	16	17	18
19	20	21	22	23	24	25
26	27	28	29	30		

JULY
M	T	W	T	F	S	S
					1	2
3	4	5	6	7	8	9
10	11	12	13	14	15	16
17	18	19	20	21	22	23
24	25	26	27	28	29	30
31						

AUGUST
M	T	W	T	F	S	S
1	2	3	4	5	6	
7	8	9	10	11	12	13
14	15	16	17	18	19	20
21	22	23	24	25	26	27
28	29	30	31			

SEPTEMBER
M	T	W	T	F	S	S
				1	2	3
4	5	6	7	8	9	10
11	12	13	14	15	16	17
18	19	20	21	22	23	24
25	26	27	28	29	30	

OCTOBER
M	T	W	T	F	S	S
						1
2	3	4	5	6	7	8
9	10	11	12	13	14	15
16	17	18	19	20	21	22
23	24	25	26	27	28	29
30	31					

NOVEMBER
M	T	W	T	F	S	S
	1	2	3	4	5	
6	7	8	9	10	11	12
13	14	15	16	17	18	19
20	21	22	23	24	25	26
27	28	29	30			

DECEMBER
M	T	W	T	F	S	S
				1	2	3
4	5	6	7	8	9	10
11	12	13	14	15	16	17
18	19	20	21	22	23	24
25	26	27	28	29	30	31

CALENDAR 2007

JANUARY
M	T	W	T	F	S	S
1	2	3	4	5	6	7
8	9	10	11	12	13	14
15	16	17	18	19	20	21
22	23	24	25	26	27	28
29	30	31				

FEBRUARY
M	T	W	T	F	S	S
			1	2	3	4
5	6	7	8	9	10	11
12	13	14	15	16	17	18
19	20	21	22	23	24	25
26	27	28				

MARCH
M	T	W	T	F	S	S
			1	2	3	4
5	6	7	8	9	10	11
12	13	14	15	16	17	18
19	20	21	22	23	24	25
26	27	28	29	30	31	

APRIL
M	T	W	T	F	S	S
						1
2	3	4	5	6	7	8
9	10	11	12	13	14	15
16	17	18	19	20	21	22
23	24	25	26	27	28	29
30						

MAY
M	T	W	T	F	S	S
	1	2	3	4	5	6
7	8	9	10	11	12	13
14	15	16	17	18	19	20
21	22	23	24	25	26	27
28	29	30	31			

JUNE
M	T	W	T	F	S	S
				1	2	3
4	5	6	7	8	9	10
11	12	13	14	15	16	17
18	19	20	21	22	23	24
25	26	27	28	29	30	

JULY
M	T	W	T	F	S	S
						1
2	3	4	5	6	7	8
9	10	11	12	13	14	15
16	17	18	19	20	21	22
23	24	25	26	27	28	29
30	31					

AUGUST
M	T	W	T	F	S	S
	1	2	3	4	5	
6	7	8	9	10	11	12
13	14	15	16	17	18	19
20	21	22	23	24	25	26
27	28	29	30	31		

SEPTEMBER
M	T	W	T	F	S	S
					1	2
3	4	5	6	7	8	9
10	11	12	13	14	15	16
17	18	19	20	21	22	23
24	25	26	27	28	29	30

OCTOBER
M	T	W	T	F	S	S
1	2	3	4	5	6	7
8	9	10	11	12	13	14
15	16	17	18	19	20	21
22	23	24	25	26	27	28
29	30	31				

NOVEMBER
M	T	W	T	F	S	S
			1	2	3	4
5	6	7	8	9	10	11
12	13	14	15	16	17	18
19	20	21	22	23	24	25
26	27	28	29	30		

DECEMBER
M	T	W	T	F	S	S
					1	2
3	4	5	6	7	8	9
10	11	12	13	14	15	16
17	18	19	20	21	22	23
24	25	26	27	28	29	30
31						

京師全圖

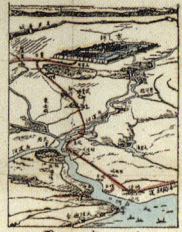

京津圖

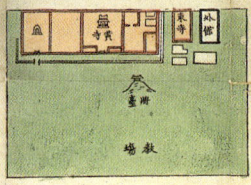

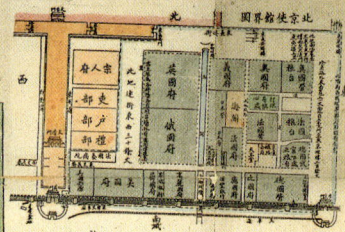

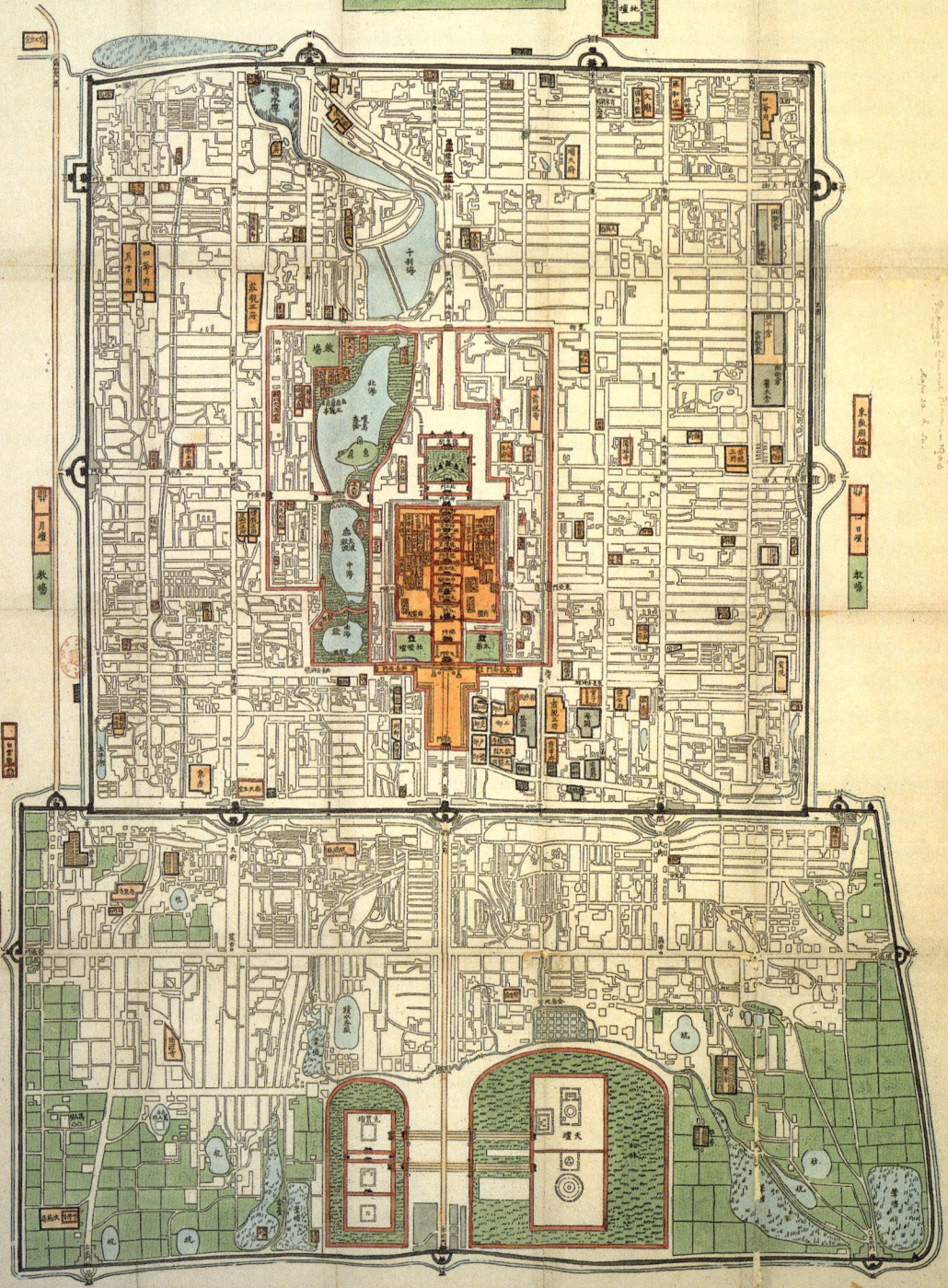

INTRODUCTION

'I am almost ashamed to say how tame and prosaic my dreams are grown. They are never romantic, seldom even rural. They are of architecture and of buildings – cities abroad which I have never seen, and hardly have hope to see. I have traversed, for the seeming length of a natural day, Rome, Amsterdam, Paris, Lisbon – their churches, palaces, squares, market-places, shops, suburbs, ruins, with an inexpressible sense of delight – a map-like distinctness of trace – and a daylight vividness of vision, that was all but being awake.'

Charles Lamb

This diary brings Lamb's dreams into the daylight and onto the page through the medium of historical maps and views. They show the historic heart of many famous cities: the ancient harbour, the hilltop fortress, the loop in the river, or the ancient shrine, and they show the houses, walls, churches and palaces which have been added over the centuries. Many of these historic maps have a pictorial quality which vanished long ago from the functional town plan: they show the principal buildings in elevation, and they show the hills or rivers against which the cities were built. Halfway between a map and a picture, they become architectural panoramas, capturing the richness of the urban fabric. Falda's Rome, Merian's Paris or Visscher's London offer us a god-like perspective on their subjects which no modern street plan can equal. It is easy to see why the perspective view flourished for so long, from the Renaissance onwards, before giving way to the scaled town plan of the age of science.

The city was linked to the birth and progress of civilisation itself, and ever since cities have acted as the focus of ideas, of arts, of sciences and of religions. They have been centres, both of ruthless imperial power and of democratic revolution. Some cities have grown slowly into a haphazard, unplanned beauty, while others have been shaped or re-shaped by the will of a masterful individual. The modern metropolis has been formed by the commercial forces which have gathered since the Industrial Revolution. Men have long searched in vain for the secret, the formula, for a great and beautiful city. They have been convinced that the city's spiritual well-being must be somehow linked to its physical form: beauty and order in the streets will inspire social harmony and individual peace – this is the ideal. It is an ideal that has been achieved again and again in the past, but which now seems to elude us. Cities have been the scene of historic events and home to all the great figures of history – artists, writers, kings, philosophers, revolutionaries and saints. This explains our love affair with the great cities of the past. Henry James wrote of Rome 'here was history in the stones of the streets and the atoms of the sunshine', and this collection of maps and views evokes precisely that sense of the richness of urban history.

Peter Whitfield

DECEMBER ✵ JANUARY

Week 52, 2005

26 *Monday*

Boxing Day (St Stephen's Day)
Holiday, UK, Republic of Ireland, Canada, USA, Australia and New Zealand (Christmas Day observed)

27 *Tuesday*

Holiday, UK, Republic of Ireland, Canada, Australia and New Zealand (Boxing Day observed)

28 *Wednesday*

29 *Thursday*

30 *Friday*

31 *Saturday*

New Year's Eve
New Moon

1 *Sunday*

New Year's Day

Seville in the early seventeenth century, seen from the south-west across the Guadalquivir. The ships moored in the river were the life-blood of Seville, the port of entry for all Spain's trade with the New World. Maps 18410 (5)

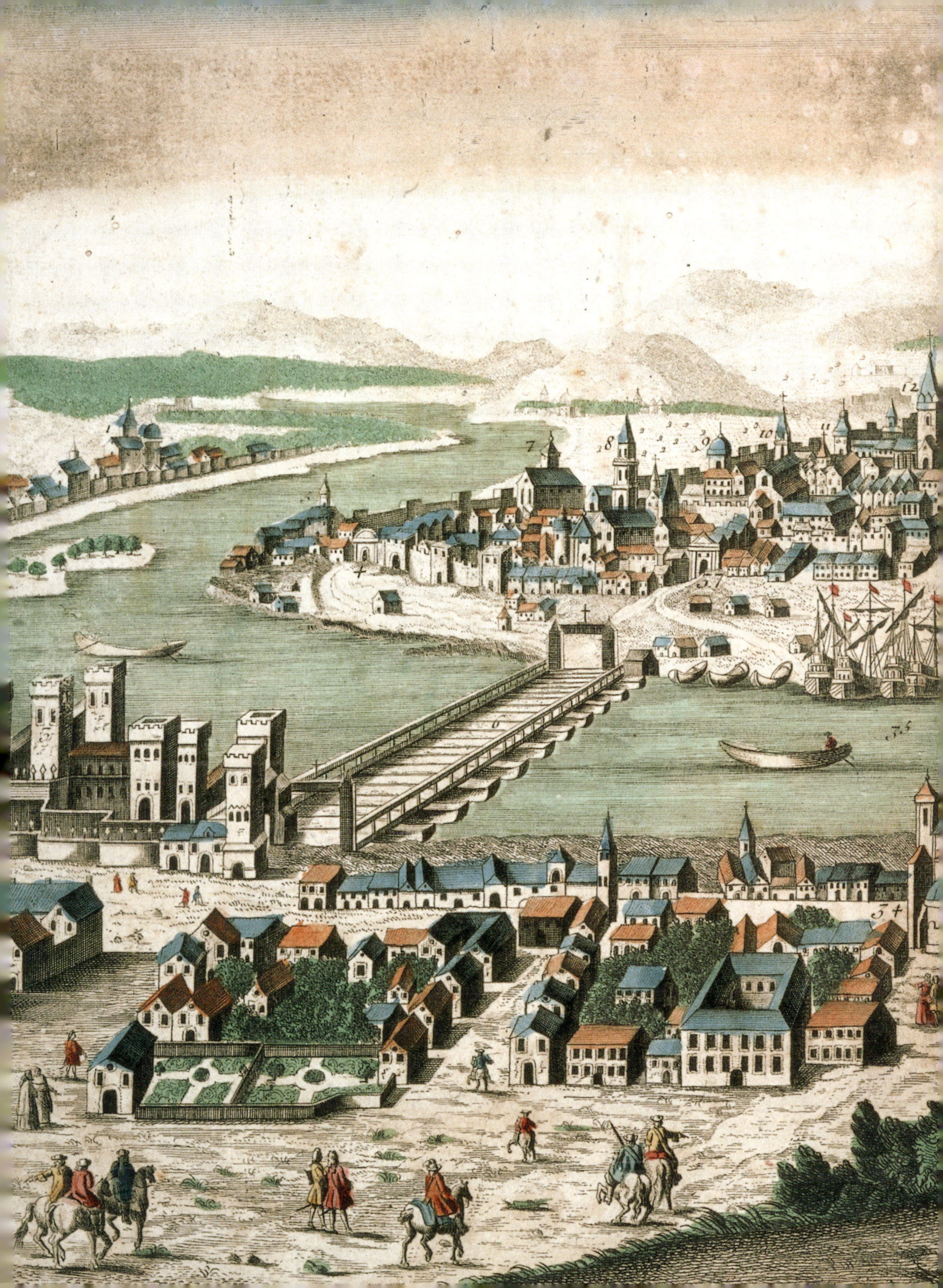

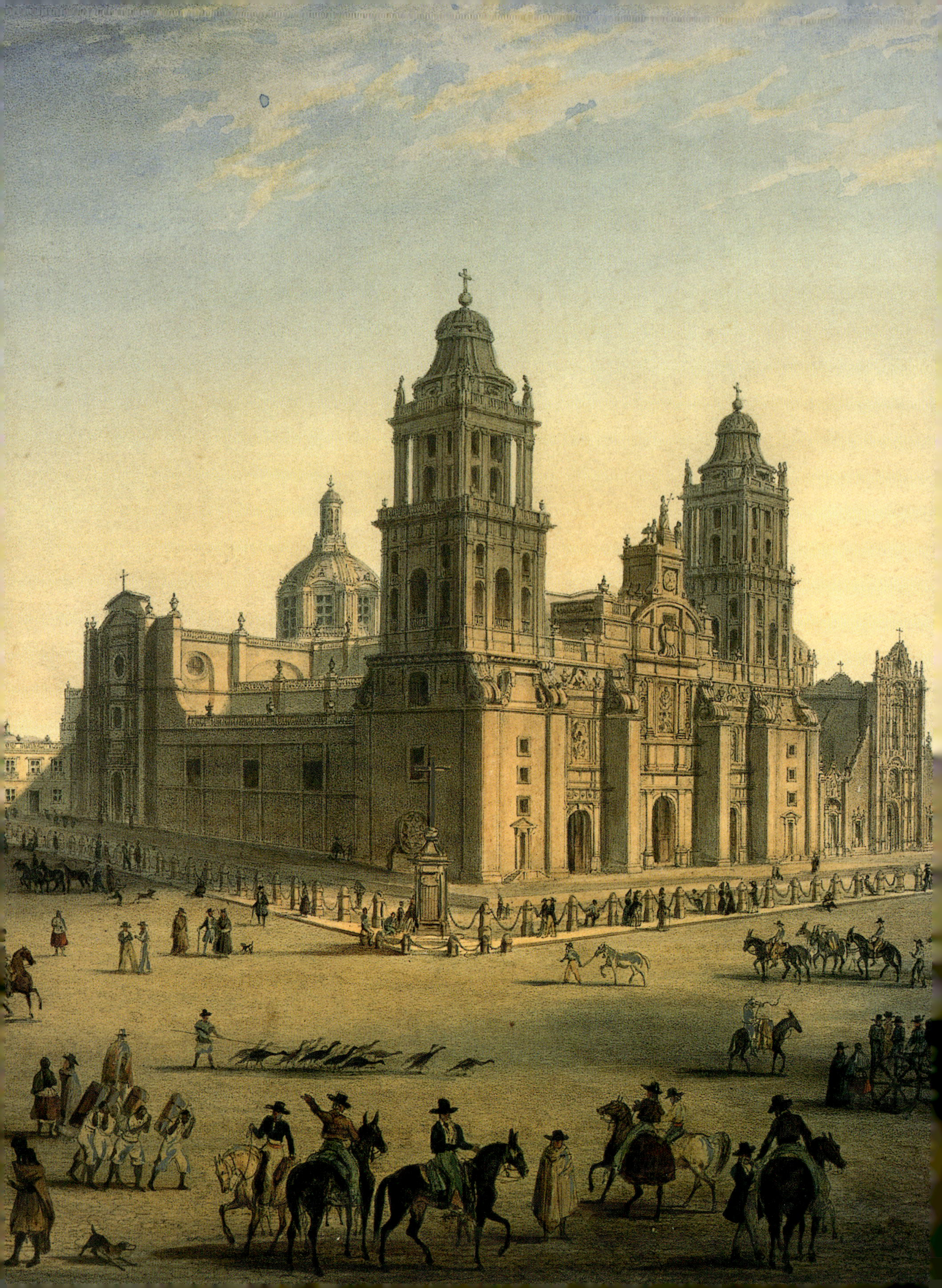

2 *Monday*   Holiday, UK, Republic of Ireland, Canada,
                                                        USA, Australia and New Zealand

3 *Tuesday*   Holiday, Scotland and New Zealand

4 *Wednesday*

5 *Thursday*

6 *Friday*   Epiphany
                                                        First Quarter

7 *Saturday*

8 *Sunday*

Mexico City in the eighteenth century, the Plaza Mayor and the baroque cathedral standing almost precisely on the site of the Aztec temple of Quetzacoatl. 648.c.1

JANUARY

9 *Monday*

10 *Tuesday*

11 *Wednesday*

12 *Thursday*

13 *Friday*

14 *Saturday*   *Full Moon*

15 *Sunday*

A tranquil view of Oxford in 1848, by Nathaniel Whittock, seen from an imaginary viewpoint above the Iffley Road.
All the classical buildings – the colleges, the Bodleian and the Ashmolean – are clearly visible, with none of the
trappings of the modern town – no traffic, no shops, no crowds. Maps 4735 (8)

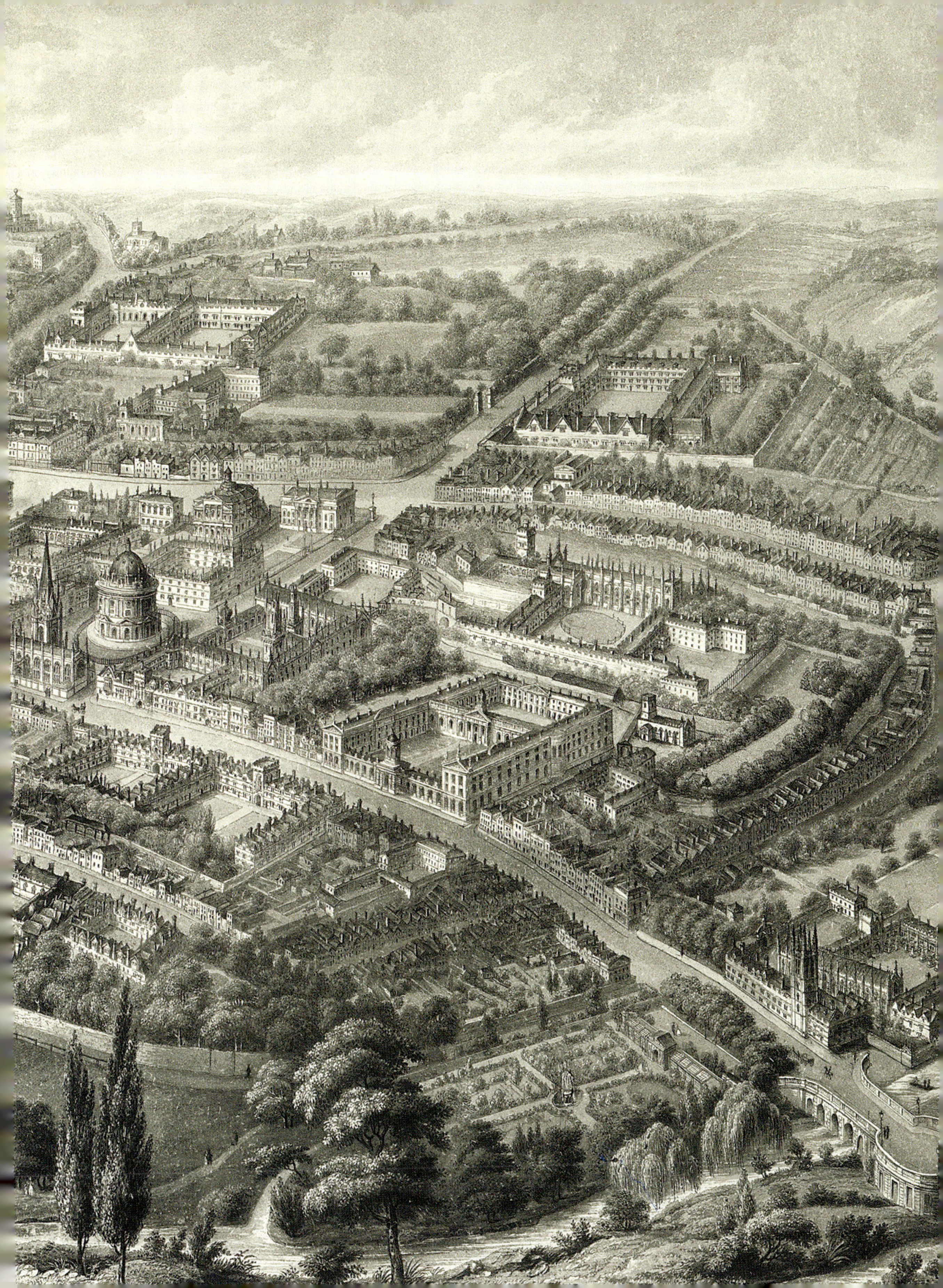

Nutt Ilaand

ye Gouernours House

Gouernours Garden

Hudſons River

THE MAINE LAND

16 *Monday*   Holiday, USA (Martin Luther King's birthday)

17 *Tuesday*

18 *Wednesday*

19 *Thursday*

20 *Friday*

21 *Saturday*

22 *Sunday*   *Last Quarter*

New York mapped in September 1661, when it was still the Dutch settlement of New Amsterdam. The protective wall where Wall Street would stand and Battery Park are both clearly visible. Maps K.Top. CXXI.35

JANUARY

23 *Monday*

24 *Tuesday*

25 *Wednesday*

26 *Thursday*   Holiday, Australia (Australia Day)

27 *Friday*

28 *Saturday*

29 *Sunday*   Chinese New Year
New Moon

An idyllic view of Sydney Cove in 1804, painted just sixteen years after the foundation of the colony, and a map
of 1854 showing the city's enormous development southwards, the docks and the newly built railways.
Maps K.Top. CXVI and Maps 90607 (18)

WOOLCOTT & CLARKE'S
MAP
OF THE
City of Sydney
with the environs of
BALMAIN AND GLEBE, CHIPPENDALE
REDFERN, PADDINGTON &c.
1854

REFERENCE

A Gipps Ward   1 Parish of St. Phillip
B Brisbane Ward   2 Parish of St. James
C Bourke Ward   3 Parish of St. Lawrence
D Macquarie Ward 4 Parish of Petersham
E Cook Ward   5 Parish of St. Andrew
F Phillip Ward   6 Parish of Alexandria

WARD BOUNDARY
PARISH BOUNDARY
Public Buildings

Eng.d by J. Carmichael, Sydney.

Accurater Grundriß und Prospect
DER KÖN. SCHWED. REICHS U. HAUPTSTADT
STOCKHOLM
mit aller herumligenden Gegend, und
annehmlicher Situation von innen u: außen.
edirt
von Ioh: Baptist: Homann
Der Röm: Kays: Maj: Geographo
in Nürnberg

30 *Monday*

31 *Tuesday*   Islamic New Year (subject to sighting of the moon)

1 *Wednesday*

2 *Thursday*

3 *Friday*

4 *Saturday*

5 *Sunday*   *First Quarter*

Stockholm c.1720. The city has the most complex geographical layout of any capital in Europe, spread over a dozen islands whose bridges and waterfronts created the image of the 'Venice of the North'. Maps K.Top. CXI.105

FEBRUARY

6 *Monday*   Holiday, New Zealand (Waitangi Day)

---

7 *Tuesday*

---

8 *Wednesday*

---

9 *Thursday*

---

10 *Friday*

---

11 *Saturday*

---

12 *Sunday*   Lincoln's birthday

Chicago. First settled in the late 1830s around a minor river mouth, the advent of the railways transformed Chicago into the massive lakeside port seen here in 1892, a freight junction between the western and eastern United States. Maps 72787 (1)

FEBRUARY

13 *Monday*

Holiday, USA (observed)
Full Moon

14 *Tuesday*

St Valentine's Day

15 *Wednesday*

16 *Thursday*

17 *Friday*

18 *Saturday*

19 *Sunday*

Arles. In the Dark Ages the ancient Roman arena was transformed into a small fortified town. 10167.aa.37

FEBRUARY

20 *Monday* — Holiday, USA (President's Day)

21 *Tuesday* — *Last Quarter*

22 *Wednesday*

23 *Thursday*

24 *Friday*

25 *Saturday*

26 *Sunday*

Moscow in 1660, drawn by the Dutch mapmaker Blaeu after a Russian original. The concentric rings of city walls which grew outwards from the Kremlin are plainly visible. Maps C.5.d.1, vol.2

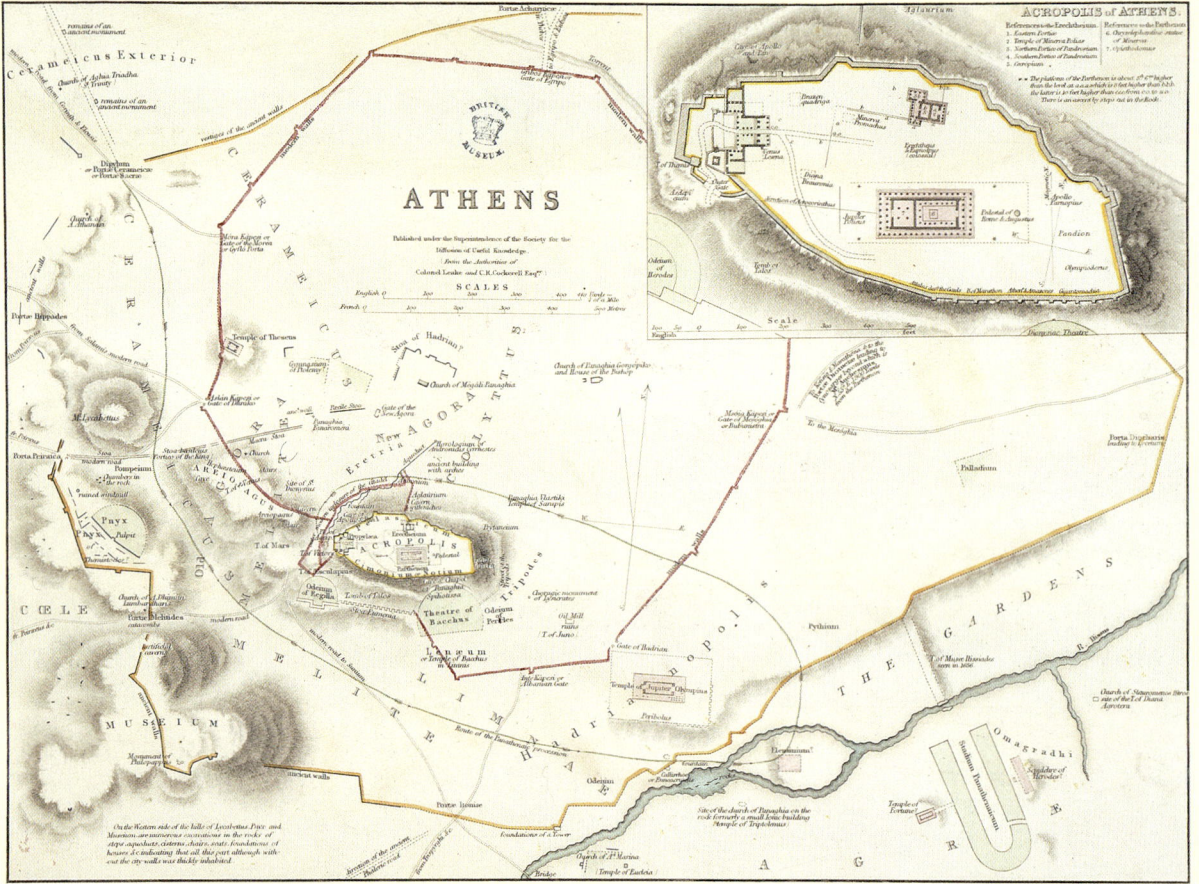

ACROPOLIS of ATHENS.

ATHENS

Published under the Superintendence of the Society for the
Diffusion of Useful Knowledge.
from the Authorities of
Colonel Leake and C.R. Cockerell Esq.

SCALES

FEBRUARY ✳ MARCH

27 *Monday*

---

28 *Tuesday*

Shrove Tuesday
New Moon

---

1 *Wednesday*

Ash Wednesday
St David's Day

---

2 *Thursday*

---

3 *Friday*

---

4 *Saturday*

---

5 *Sunday*

Athens, a map of the classical sites published in 1844, and a view of the Acropolis looking out across near-deserted countryside and a few unimportant dwellings. Maps 38.e.8 and Tab 1237.a

MARCH

6 *Monday* *First Quarter*

7 *Tuesday*

8 *Wednesday*

9 *Thursday*

10 *Friday*

11 *Saturday*

12 *Sunday*

Helsingor, c.1660, by de Wit. The Kronborg – 'Hamlet's Castle' – overlooks the narrow strait between Denmark and Sweden. The small island of Hvena was the site of Tycho Brahe's great observatory. Maps C.10.e.14 (117)

FRETI DANICI OR SVNDT
ACCVRATISS DELINEATIO.

HELSEBVRGVM

LANDESKRON

HVENA

Vraniburgum

LISSI MVM DANIAE F

CORONEBVRGV

HELSCHENOR

Lundehoue

Cambridge

The Head Quarters of the Rebels

Mount Pisgah or Prospect Hill

Middle Hill

Plough'd Hill

Winter Hill

Mystick River

Penny Ferry

Lines & Redoubts thrown up by our Troops after y.e Victory on 8.17 June 1775.

Charlestown Neck

Gondoles

Artillery

Gen.l Howe's Camp

BUNKERS HILL

Redoubt taken from y.e Rebels by Gen.l Howe

Dragoons

A Pond

Marines

CHARLESTOWN

Troops Landed 17 June under General Howe

Charlestown Point

River Charles or Cambridge River

Jersey Point to defend y.e Entrance

Phipps's Farm

Willis's Creek

Bartons Point

Royal Irish

Mount Whoredom

Mill Dam

Mill Pond

North End

Church Yard

N

Fox Hill Battery

Common

Beacon Hill

Artillery

Encamp.t of 6 Reg.t

Hannover Str.

Middle Str.

B

Gondole

BOSTON

Newberry Str.

Marlborough Str.

C

Pond

T

Wharf

Charles's Wharf

Boston Neck

ORANGE STREET

ORANGE STR.

G

Windmill Point

F

Old Wharf

Long Wharf

Boston Harbour

B

N.

I

H

FOSTER NECK

Foster Hill

Signal Tree Hill

Bush Tree Hill

Williams's House burnt by y.e Rebels

NODDLES

This Shoal and all the rest thus Shaded are Dry at Low Water

Dorchester Point

Bird I.

Castle Island

Governor's Island

MARCH

13 *Monday*   Commonwealth Day

14 *Tuesday*   *Full Moon*

15 *Wednesday*

16 *Thursday*

17 *Friday*   St Patrick's Day
Holiday, Northern Ireland and Republic of Ireland

18 *Saturday*

19 *Sunday*

Boston, a plan published at the outbreak of the War of Independence in 1776, clearly showing the city's original island character, later obscured by infilling of the harbour. Maps 1. Tab.44 (17)

MARCH

20 *Monday*   Vernal Equinox

21 *Tuesday*

22 *Wednesday*   *Last Quarter*

23 *Thursday*

24 *Friday*

25 *Saturday*

26 *Sunday*   Mothering Sunday, UK
British Summertime begins

Genoa, one of the vivid but inaccurate woodcut views of European cities published in the *Nuremberg Chronicle* of 1493. IB 6422

27 *Monday*

28 *Tuesday*

29 *Wednesday*   *New Moon*

30 *Thursday*

31 *Friday*

1 *Saturday*

2 *Sunday*

Nagasaki, a Japanese woodcut map c.1680. The small curved island in the centre is Deshima, the Dutch trading post which was the sole permitted point of contact between Japan and the Europeans. Maps 63055 (2)

APRIL

3 *Monday*

4 *Tuesday*

5 *Wednesday*   *First Quarter*

6 *Thursday*

7 *Friday*

8 *Saturday*

9 *Sunday*   Palm Sunday

Palmanova, the archetypal planned, symmetrical city of the Renaissance, built by the Venetians as a defensive fortress against the Austrians, and completed in 1603. Maps C.29.e.1

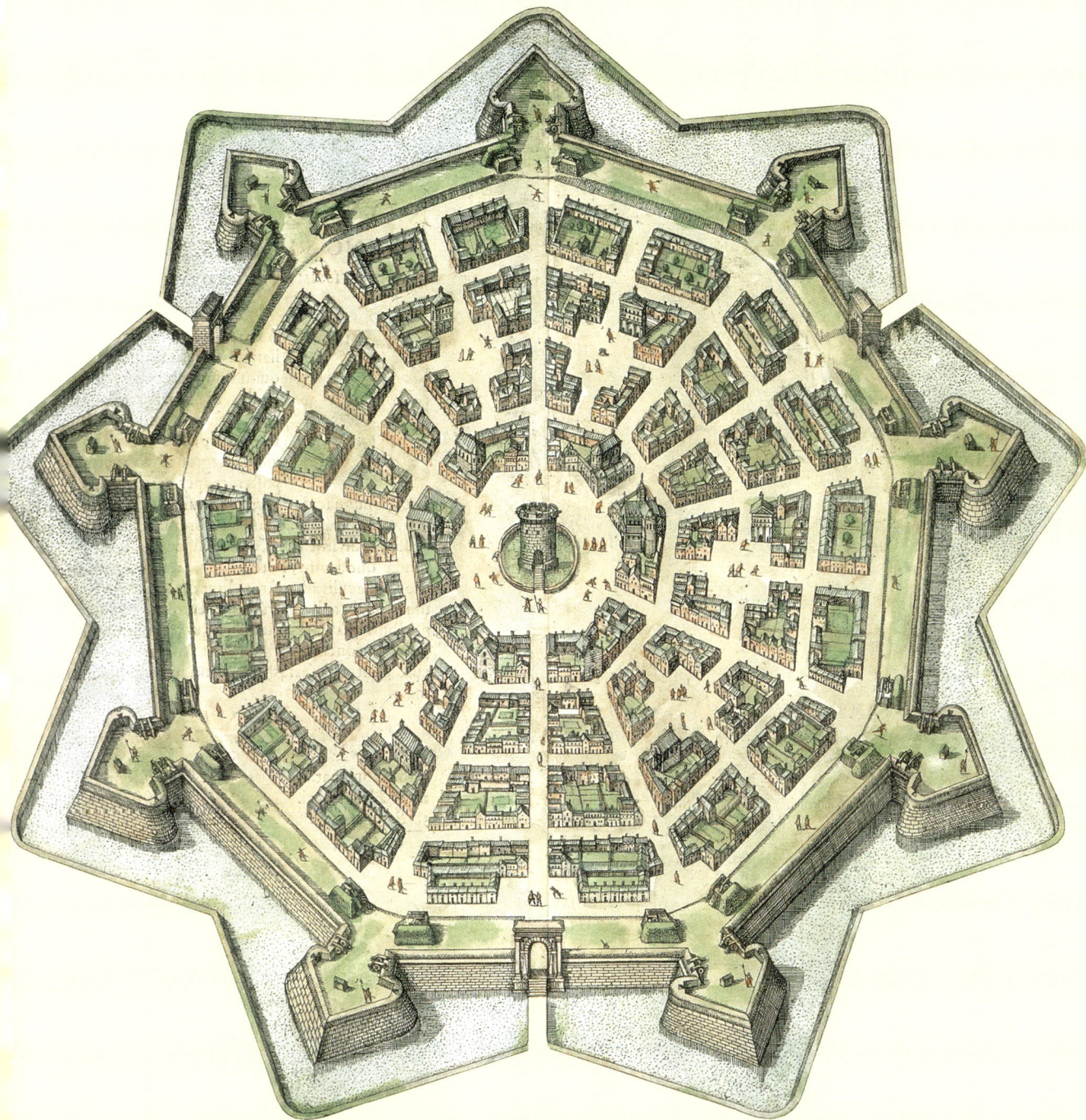

APRIL

10 *Monday*

11 *Tuesday*

12 *Wednesday*

13 *Thursday*

Maundy Thursday
Passover (Pesach), First Day
Full Moon

14 *Friday*

Good Friday
Holiday, UK, Republic of Ireland,
Canada, USA, Australia and New Zealand

15 *Saturday*

16 *Sunday*

Easter Sunday

Bath c.1800. With its hillside setting and elegant Georgian architecture, Bath was a uniquely picturesque subject for artists. 199.i.7

APRIL

17 *Monday*

Easter Monday
Holiday, UK (exc. Scotland), Republic of Ireland,
Canada, Australia and New Zealand

---

18 *Tuesday*

---

19 *Wednesday*

Passover (Pesach), Seventh Day

---

20 *Thursday*

Passover (Pesach), Eighth Day

---

21 *Friday*

Birthday of Queen Elizabeth II
Last Quarter

---

22 *Saturday*

---

23 *Sunday*

St George's Day

Bristol c.1710, showing the inner city as virtually a peninsula between the Avon and the Frome: a medieval chronicler had written 'the whole city seems to swim on the water and sit on its banks'. Maps K.Top. XXXVII.32

AN EXACT DELINEATION OF THE FAMOUS CITTY OF BRISTOL

together with all the High wayes, through fares, streets, lanes, and publick passages, therein Contained, Composed by a Scale Ichnographically Described Engraven & Published by V.

Branden Hill
Instar solis micas spectator
Collis hic Instans unstis
meos solet

The Hill is a publick conveniency
to ij Citty for ij use of dry
ing Cloaths

The Park

At Conduit head

Little Park

Washingtones Breach

The Royal Fort

Stony hill

The Bishope Park

Frog lane

The Colledge Greene

The Cathedrall

The Queens Square

Chanons Marsh

Glassehouse

Redland Hill

Mary Redliff

Redliff Mead

Temple Church

Temple Meade

The Rack Closes

The brick kilne

Kingsmarsh

Broad Mead

The Horse faire

Castle gate

BRISTOLIA

Congestæ Urbis nimium mirere congeribus alti...
Fessaq et fessas undiq perterea capit...
Has iterum crescunt occidentes ornamina campi...
Et sæta quæ Cereris munere præssa patent...
Fœta replent passi quæ rupibus horrida vallis...
Vel solvi nulla fœda pudebi sonat...
In medio duplicem sedet Urbs celeberrima portum...
Turrigerum tollens culmen in astra suum...
Extendens binos super amnes amula pontes...
Tremulum magnis flumina magna premens...
Vela binæ dant arcus rupestia turbida puppes...
Huc iterum plaudis Classis vivida redit...
Huc Orienis merces, merces Occidui et Omni...
Itur mare, per ventos advehit Orbis opes...
Unde sit Emporium cui qui commercia callent...
Emptors propterunt undiq turba virum...
In pamisfiq fiæt restituens omnibus Urbis...
Præstantis narrant non mediocre decus...
Cuncta, miventes quibus haud festantur ocelli...
Bristoliæ dicunt non reticendus honos...
Urbs omnis celebri spatiosa fiddis amans...
Dulce de iniquis propera bonigna intens...
Iura Dcoum Regeren, Regimenta Crimina Favere...
Servet adesse amat proregem Gelet Habet...

A Sᵗ Nicholas gate and Church
B The High Crosse
C The Tolzey
D All Saints Church
E Sᵗ Werburge Church and Church
F Sᵗ Leonards gate and Church
G The present Custom House
H Sᵗ Giles gate and Church
I Sᵗ Iohns gate and Church
L The Guild Hall
M Sᵗ Ewins Church
N Christ Church
O The Market house
P The Meale market
Q The Grener schoole
R Christmas street

Created by Iohn Groten at the White horse without Newgate London, And by Thomas Wall Bookseller in Bristoll.

The Corne Market-house in Wine streete Bristoll

A Grounde plat of the Royall Fort on ij Northwest side of Bristoll built by his High P Rupert. An Dom 1644

The Fort being now converted into house and pleasant gardens, demolished

The North prospect of Sᵗ Austins horn Colstons

The Scale of yards

An English Mile Containeth 1760 yards.

CVSCO. REGNI PERV IN NOVO ORBE CAPVT.

APRIL

24 *Monday*

25 *Tuesday*   Holiday, Australia and New Zealand (Anzac Day)

26 *Wednesday*

27 *Thursday*   *New Moon*

28 *Friday*

29 *Saturday*

30 *Sunday*

Cuzco, a view published in 1572. This is a version of the only image of the ancient Inca capital available to Europeans, probably not very accurate but much copied. In reality the city must have been much larger and less regular. The Temple of the Sun is on the left. Maps C.29.e.1 (1)

MAY

1 *Monday*   Early May Bank Holiday, UK and Republic of Ireland

2 *Tuesday*

3 *Wednesday*

4 *Thursday*

5 *Friday*   *First Quarter*

6 *Saturday*

7 *Sunday*

Paris in 1650 by Merian. The classic view from the west with the great wall on the left linking the old fortresses, the Louvre and the Bastille, and the Isle de la Cité as the central focus. Maps 152.d.4

Charenton

Conflan

Butte Cypres

Porte S. Antoine

La Bastille

R. S. Antoine

P. S. Paul

P. St. Bernard

Place Maubert

Place de Greve

P. de Greve

Les Halles

LA RIVIERE DE SEINE

La pute   Le pont neuf

Faubourg St. Henri

Les Capucins

8 *Monday*

9 *Tuesday*

10 *Wednesday*

11 *Thursday*

12 *Friday*

13 *Saturday* *Full Moon*

14 *Sunday* Mother's Day, Canada, USA, Australia and New Zealand

Nimrud, a romanticized reconstruction of the ancient Assyrian capital on the River Tigris. Cup 648.c.2, pl.1

MAY

15 *Monday*

16 *Tuesday*

17 *Wednesday*

18 *Thursday*

19 *Friday*

20 *Saturday*   *Last Quarter*

21 *Sunday*

Bern (above) in 1653, seen from the south, tightly confined in the loop of the River Aare, and fortified on the east. Zurich (below) stands where the River Limnat flows out from the lake, with its famous Rathaus built on the bridge. Maps 24845 (1) and Maps 26735 (13)

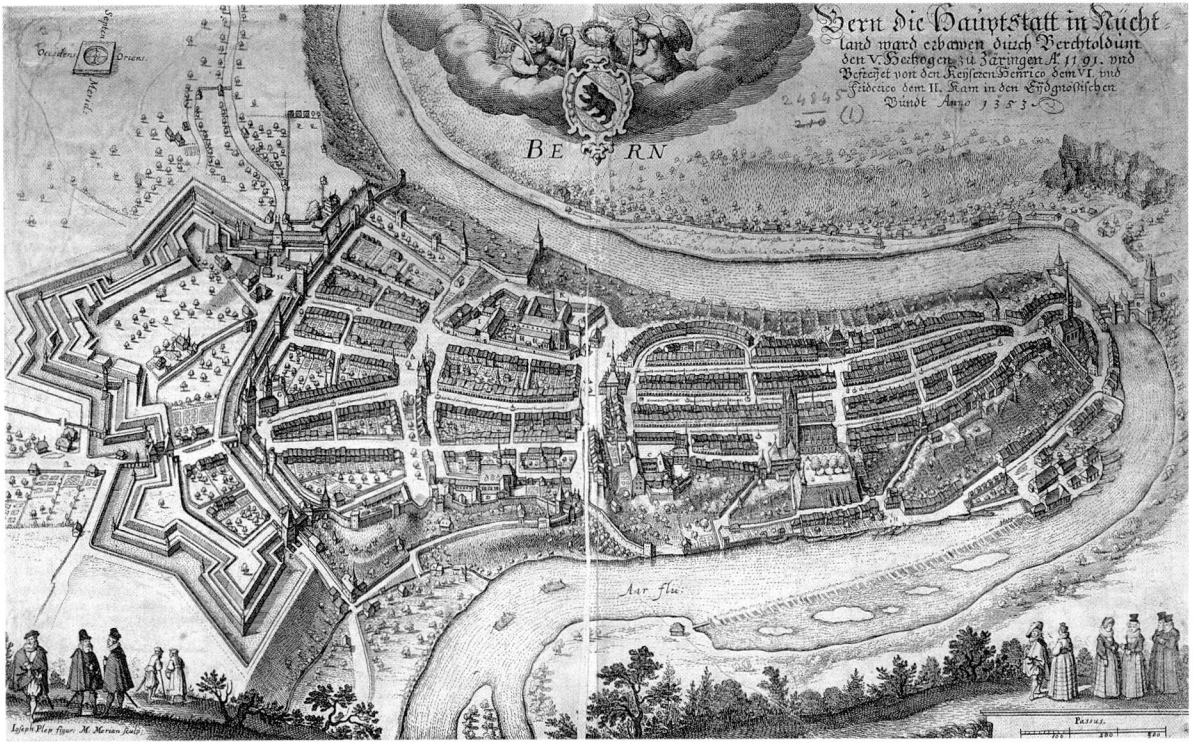

BE RN

Bern die Hauptstatt in Nucht
land ward erbawen durch Perchtoldum
den V. Hertzogen zu Zäringen A° 1191. vnd
befreyet von den Keyseren Henrico dem VI. vnd
Friderico dem II. Kam in den Eydgnossischen
Bundt Anno 1353

Aar flu:

Ioseph Plep figur. M. Merian Sculp.

Passus

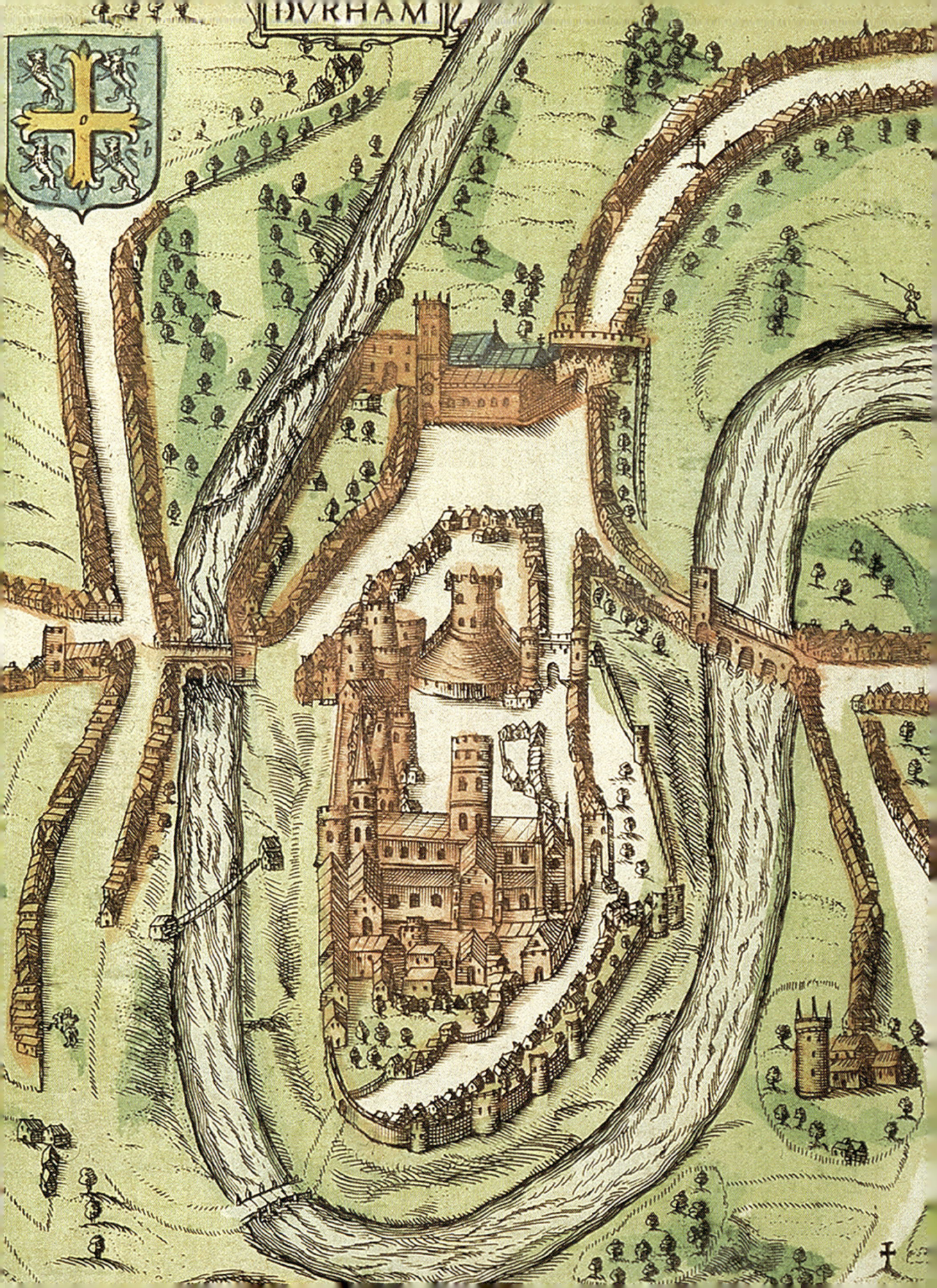

DVRHAM

22 *Monday*

23 *Tuesday*

24 *Wednesday*

25 *Thursday*   Ascension Day

26 *Friday*

27 *Saturday*   *New Moon*

28 *Sunday*

Durham, by John Speed, 1611. The castle and cathedral are islanded in the River Wear, and this has ensured great historical continuity: development is possible only outside the old city. Maps C.7.c.20

MAY ✳ JUNE

29 *Monday*   Spring Bank Holiday, UK
                                   Holiday, USA (Memorial Day)

30 *Tuesday*

31 *Wednesday*

1 *Thursday*

2 *Friday*   Jewish Feast of Weeks (Shavuot)

3 *Saturday*   *First Quarter*

4 *Sunday*   Whit Sunday (Pentecost)

.

Delhi in 1851, still a compact city, dominated by the Jami Masjid Mosque and the Red Fort, and not yet the capital of the Raj. The lower view shows the Yamuna River and Red Fort, built by Shah Jehan in the mid-seventeenth century. Maps 55455 (1) and Cup 652.m.34

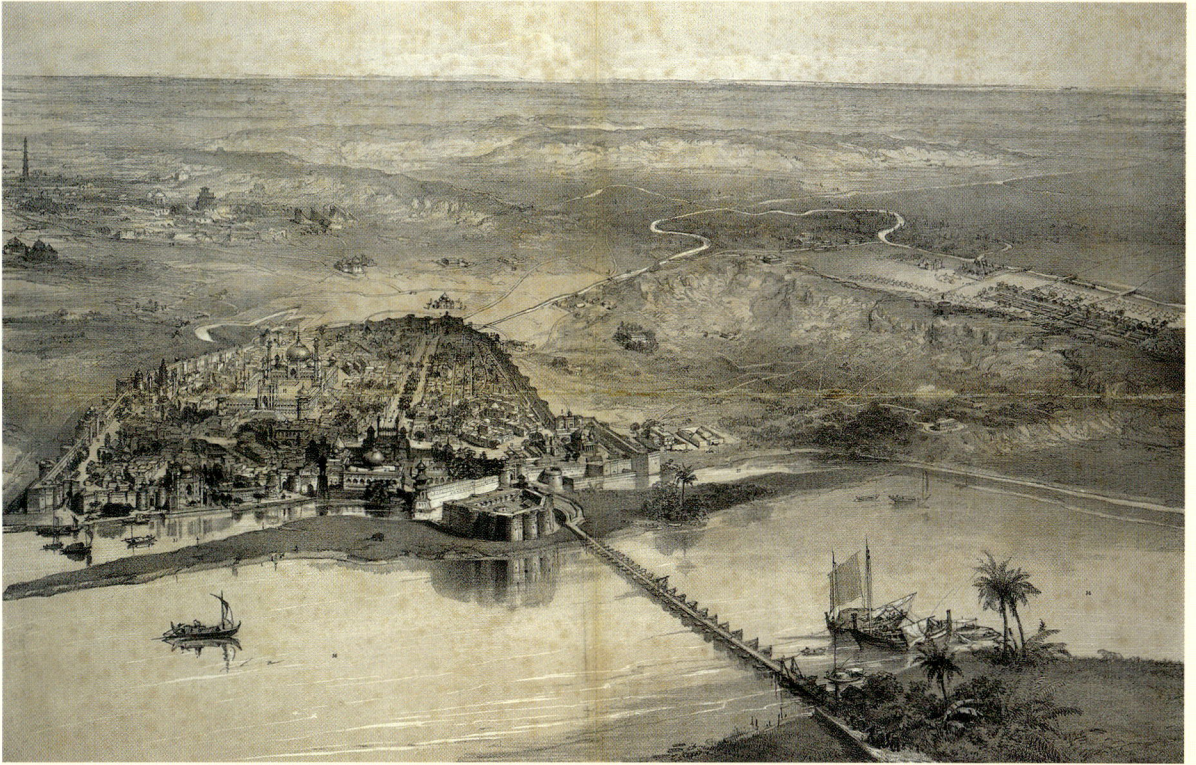

OCCIDENS (left margin) — **ORIENS** (right margin) — **MERIDIES** (bottom margin)

CANTEBRIGIA, Vrbs celeberrima a Granta fluuio vicino, Cairgrant
a primo non tam vrbis quam Academiæ conditore Cantabro, magni nominis Hispano,
Cantebrigia, a Saxonibus Grauntecestre, et Grantebrige iam olim nuncupata est. Fluuius ho-
die antiquum nomen retinens, flexuosis riparum anfractibus ab austro in aquilonem mari tenus
longissimo tractu protenditur Vrbi vero conditoris nomen et memoriam sempiternam reddens
etiam Academiæ dignitatem multo quam olim fuit illustriorem conseruat Muro fuisse cinc-
tam historiæ referunt sed eum pictis Danicis et Saxonicis bellis (ut et veterem vrbis faciem)
concidisse Henricus tertius Angliæ Rex circa annū Dñi 1265. fossa et portis Cantebrigiam
muniuit Quo tempore ibim contra exheredatorū iniurias et excursiones, q Eliensem Insulam
occupabant se defendit Muro etiam iam tum rursus cinxisset, nisi eo absente Londino a
Gilberto Clarensi duce occupato, nouæ calamitati prospicere fuisset coactus huic fossæ q
ab eo tempore Regiæ nomen obtinuit vestigia quædam in hac charta cernitur Sed q
ad vrbis ambitū et defensionē altissimus, fuit, et latissimus fossionibus primum apparata
expurgandis platearū sordib eundis, in grātā fluuiū sordibz non male nunc inseruit Q
si Cantebrigienses coniunctis opib efficerent, vt q est ad vadū Trumpingtoniæ amniculus
fossam hanc allueret, non esset Cantebrigia vrbs vlla elegantior, tantiq facti memoria non
tam posteris grata quam ipsis iucunda et fructuosa existeret.

Castell

Parochia ... ad ... Castellum

S. Petri

Magdalen Colledge

The Bridge

S. Clemens

Iesus Colledge

Barnwell cawsey

Trinitie Coll.
Trinitie Coll. Chap.

Garret Ostell greene

Michaelhouse

Grey Friers

Trinitie Hall
Clare Hall

Gunwell
Benney

Gonivell

Kinges Colledge Chappell

White Friers

Queene Coll.

Newnam
Kinges mill

Pembroke hall

S. Thomas Leys

Peterhouse

ACADEMIÆ · OPPIDI

RIC. LYNE SCVLPSIT

Aº DÑI 1574

MAT — CANT

HOSPITIA ARCIS TAR.

A — Kinges Hall
B — Michaell house
C — Phisnicke Ostell
D — Gregorye Ostell
E — Garet Ostell
F — Sᵗ Marie Ostell
G — Sᵗ Austines Ostell
H — Bernarde Ostell
K — Sᵗ Thomas Ostell
— Rudolph Ostell

HOSPITIA IVRISTARVM

L — Ouins Inn
M — Paules Inn
N — Clemens Ostell
O — Trinitie Ostell
P — Sᵗ Nicholas Ostell
Q — Burden Ostell
R — Domus Pythagoræ
S — Dᵒ Sᵗ Bedæ
T — Crates ferrea vbi olim pons
Canteber a Cantebri vnde Cantebrigia.

5 *Monday*   Holiday, Republic of Ireland
Holiday, New Zealand (The Queen's birthday)

6 *Tuesday*

7 *Wednesday*

8 *Thursday*

9 *Friday*

10 *Saturday*   The Queen's official birthday (subject to confirmation)

11 *Sunday*   Trinity Sunday
Full Moon

Cambridge, drawn in 1547 by Richard Lyne. The layout of the inner city is unchanged, but most of the colleges have been rebuilt on classical lines. Maps C.24.a.27

JUNE

12 *Monday*   Holiday, Australia (The Queen's birthday)

13 *Tuesday*

14 *Wednesday*

15 *Thursday*   Corpus Christi

16 *Friday*

17 *Saturday*

18 *Sunday*   Father's Day, UK, Canada and USA
Last Quarter

London, Ludgate Hill and St Paul's in 1860; one of Gustave Doré's engravings of the dark, seething mass that nineteenth-century London had become. 1788.b.20

JUNE

19 *Monday*

20 *Tuesday*

21 *Wednesday* Summer Solstice

22 *Thursday*

23 *Friday*

24 *Saturday*

25 *Sunday* *New Moon*

Seville in the early seventeenth century, the great Cathedral with its tower – the Giralda – once the minaret of the city's mosque, and the Moorish 'Golden Tower', seen across the Gualdalquivir. Maps 18410 (5)

26 *Monday*

27 *Tuesday*

28 *Wednesday*

29 *Thursday*

30 *Friday*

1 *Saturday*   Holiday, Canada (Canada Day)

2 *Sunday*

Azilia, the fantasy city designed by Sir Robert Montgomery in 1717 as a proposed new colony to be established in Georgia, but never built. It was to be exactly twenty miles square, defended by great walls, and to contain 116 individual estates, each exactly one mile square. 103.k.34

A *Plan representing the Form* of *Setling the Districts,* or *County Divisions in* the *Margravate of Azilia.*

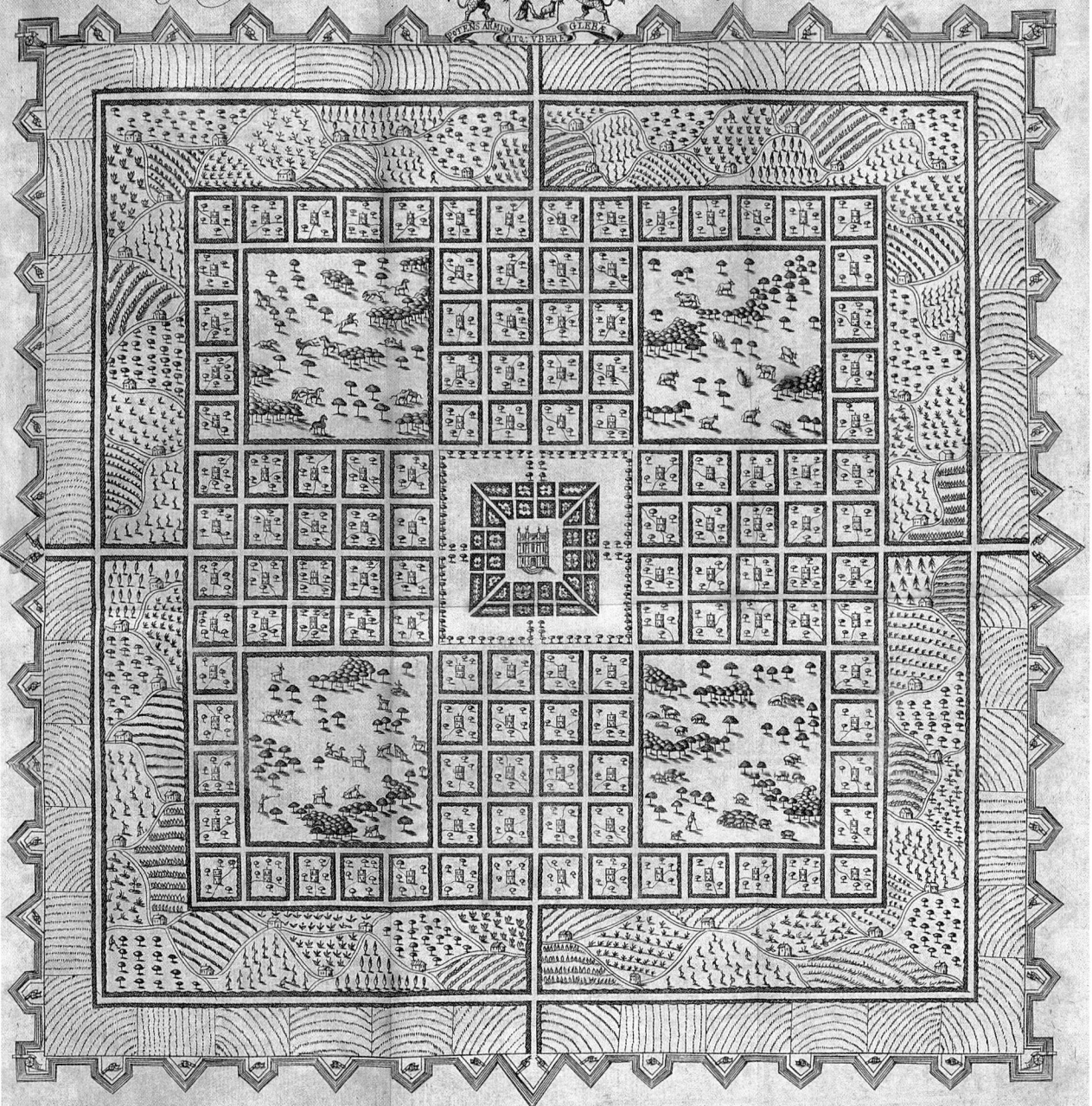

OYSTER BANKS

Buckingham Island

PART OF NEW JERSEY

To His Excellency Sir Henry Moore Bart.
Captain General and Governour in Chief
In and Over His Majesty's Province of
NEW YORK
This PLAN
of the City of New York and its Environs
is humbly dedicated by His Excellency's
most Obedient and most humble Servant
B. Ratzer

Magnetick Meridian

PAULUS HOOK

Southward Boundaries

NORTH OR HUDSON'S RIVER

Westward Boundaries

The WALLABOUT BAY

EAST RIVER OR THE SOUND

OR LONG ISLAND

JULY

3 *Monday* *First Quarter*

4 *Tuesday* Holiday, USA (Independence Day)

5 *Wednesday*

6 *Thursday*

7 *Friday*

8 *Saturday*

9 *Sunday*

New York – Manhattan Island – drawn by a British survey officer, and published in 1776, just weeks before much of the city was destroyed by fire at the outbreak of the War of Independence. Maps 1. Tab.44 (28)

JULY

10 *Monday*

11 *Tuesday*   *Full Moon*

12 *Wednesday*   Holiday, Northern Ireland (Battle of the Boyne)

13 *Thursday*

14 *Friday*

15 *Saturday*   St Swithin's Day

16 *Sunday*

Marseille at the beginning of the seventeenth century, looking west across the old port to the basilica of Notre Dame de la Garde. Across the open fields in the foreground runs the boulevard of La Canebiere. Add. MS 21117, ff.94v–5

Nre Dame de la garde.

Le Port,

PERA

CONSTAN=
TINOPOLIS.

porta delmeso

Sctã demeÿ

Sctã geor
gius

Turqui

chiramea

portus olim
pilaaÿ im
patoris

Palaciū Imperatoris

Scã Johes d petri

porta

predomus

palaciū impatoris

Calchidon

Scã Johes d
andi

olangu

portus sed destruit
precepto teutroÿ

Saita

JULY

17 *Monday*

18 *Tuesday*

19 *Wednesday*

20 *Thursday*

21 *Friday*

22 *Saturday*

23 *Sunday*

Constantinople, a medieval manuscript painting showing the Christian city, with Hagia Sophia prominent on the right, and many Roman remains. The commercial quarter of Pera lies across the Golden Horn. Arundel MS 93, f.155

JULY

24 *Monday*

25 *Tuesday*   *New Moon*

26 *Wednesday*

27 *Thursday*

28 *Friday*

29 *Saturday*

30 *Sunday*

Rome, the great panoramic map of 1676 by Falda, showing all the buildings in elevation. This pictorial style of urban mapping was soon to be replaced by the more functional scale plan. Maps 3.e.22

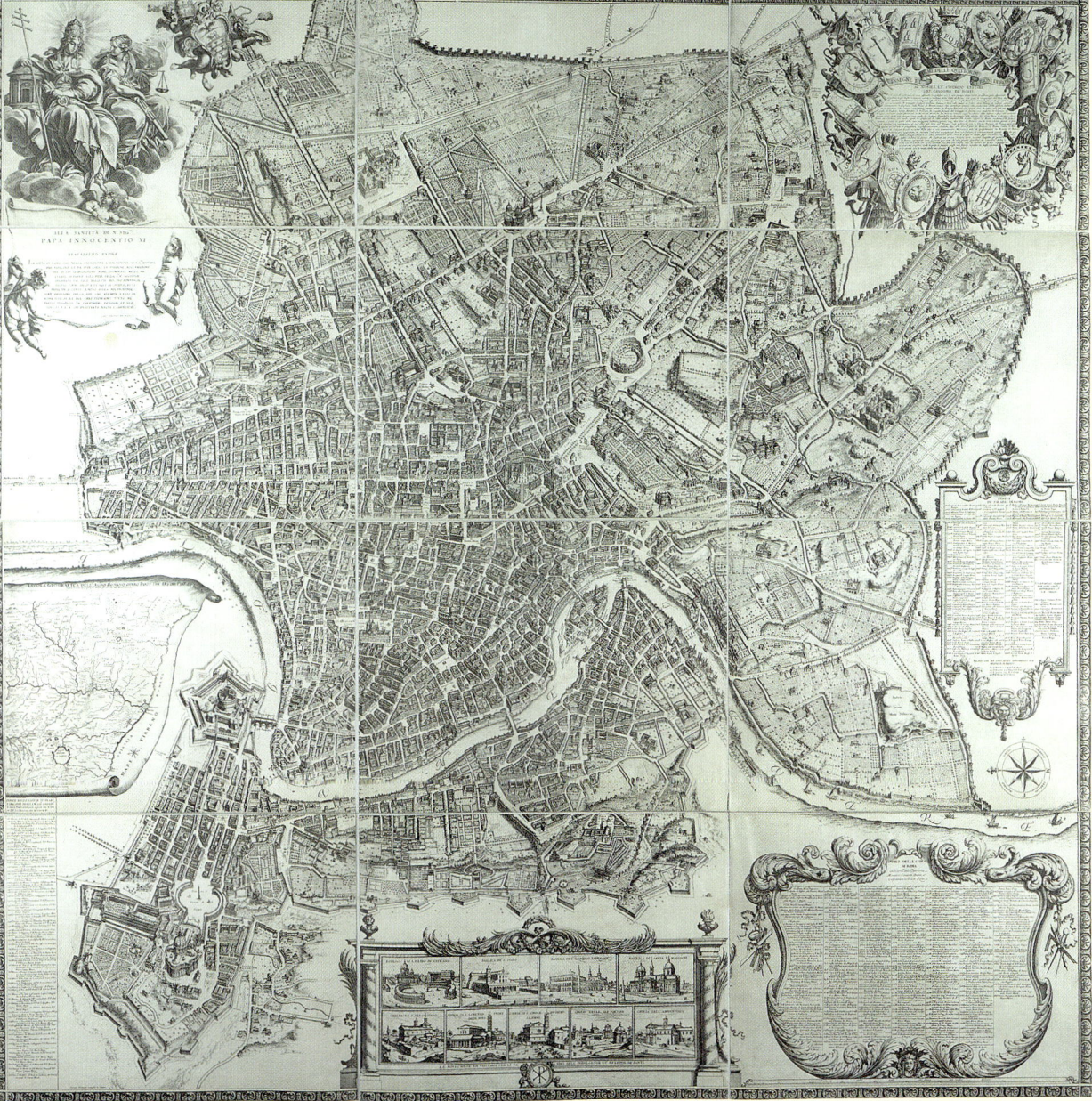

NVOVA PIANTA ET ALZATA DELLA CITTA DI ROMA CON TVTTE LE STRADE PIAZZE ET EDIFICII DE TEMPII

PALAZZI GIARDINI ET ALTRE FABBRICHE ANTICHE E MODERNE, COME SI TROVANO AL PRESENTE NEL PONTIFICATO DI N.S. PAPA INNOCENTIO XI. CON LE LORO DICHIARATIONI NOMI ET INDICE COPIO

SISSIMO DISEGNIATA ET INTAGLIATA DA GIO. BATTISTA FALDA DA VALDVEGGIA ET DATE AL PVBLICO DA GIO. GIACOMO DE ROSSI DALLE SVE STAMPE IN ROMA ALLA PACE L'ANNO 1676 CON PRIVILEGGIO DEL SOM. PONT

PAPA INNOCENTIO XI

JULY ✸ AUGUST

31 *Monday*

1 *Tuesday*

2 *Wednesday*   *First Quarter*

3 *Thursday*

4 *Friday*

5 *Saturday*

6 *Sunday*

Nimrud, an imaginary view of the Assyrian capital. The famous winged bulls can be seen decorating the walls of the palace. Cup 648.c.2, pl.1

AUGUST

7 *Monday*   Summer Bank Holiday, Scotland and Republic of Ireland

---

8 *Tuesday*

---

9 *Wednesday*   *Full Moon*

---

10 *Thursday*

---

11 *Friday*

---

12 *Saturday*

---

13 *Sunday*

London, showing (above) the devastation of the Great Fire of 1666, and (below) the city just ten years later
'now rebuilt since the late dreadfull Fire', with its street lines unchanged. Maps Crace 1.50 and Maps 1. Tab.18 (4)

AN EXACT SVRVEIGH OF THE STREETS LANES AND CHVRCHES CONTAINED WITHIN THE RVINES OF THE CITY OF LONDON FIRST DESCRIBED IN SIX PLATS. BY IOHN LEAKE. IOHN
IENNINGS, WILLIAM MARR, WILL. LEYBVRN, THOMAS STREETE, & RICHARD SHORTGRAVE in Dec.br A. 1666. BY THE ORDER OF THE LORD MAIOR, ALDERMEN, AND COMMON COVNCELL OF THE SAID CITY

The Prospect of this Citty, as it appeared from the opposite Southwarke side, in the fire time.

THE RIVER THA MES

A Mapp of the Cityes of LONDON & WESTMINSTER & Burrough of SOUTHWARK with their Suburbs as it is now Rebult since the late dreadfull Fire

SOUTHWARK

GOA·

MORM

CABO

BARDES

AGO

AUGUST

14 *Monday*

---

15 *Tuesday*

---

16 *Wednesday*   *Last Quarter*

---

17 *Thursday*

---

18 *Friday*

---

19 *Saturday*

---

20 *Sunday*

Goa, a Portuguese view of the island city painted in 1646, with north at the bottom. The naïve use of multiple perspectives suggests that this colourful image may have been based on an Indian original. Sloane MS 197, ff.247v–8

AUGUST

21 *Monday*

22 *Tuesday*

23 *Wednesday*   *New Moon*

24 *Thursday*

25 *Friday*

26 *Saturday*

27 *Sunday*

Mexico. The Aztec city of Tenochtitlan amazed the conquistadors, with its temples and palaces built on islands in a great lake, like Venice. Their admiration did not prevent their destroying it however, and when this drawing was published in 1556, it no longer existed. 566.k.1–3

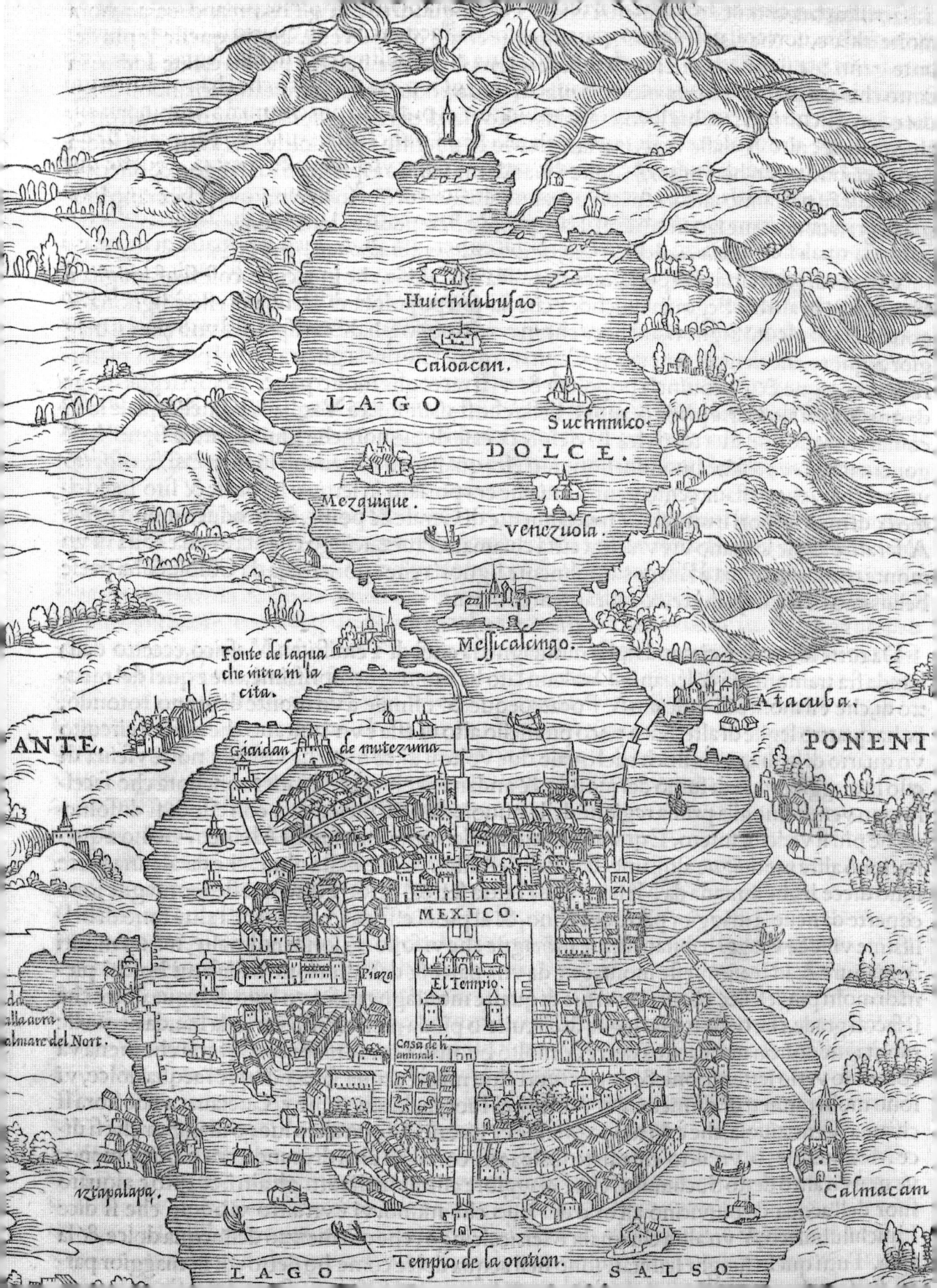

Huichilubufao

Caloacan.

LAGO

DOLCE

Suchmilco

Mezquique.

venezuola.

Meſſicalcingo.

Fonte de laqua
che intra in la
cita.

ANTE.

Giardan de mutezuma

Atacuba.

PONENT

MEXICO.

PIA
ZA

Piaza

El Tempio.

Caſa de li
animali.

del Nort.

iztapalapa.

Calmacam.

LAGO   Tempio de la oration.   SALSO

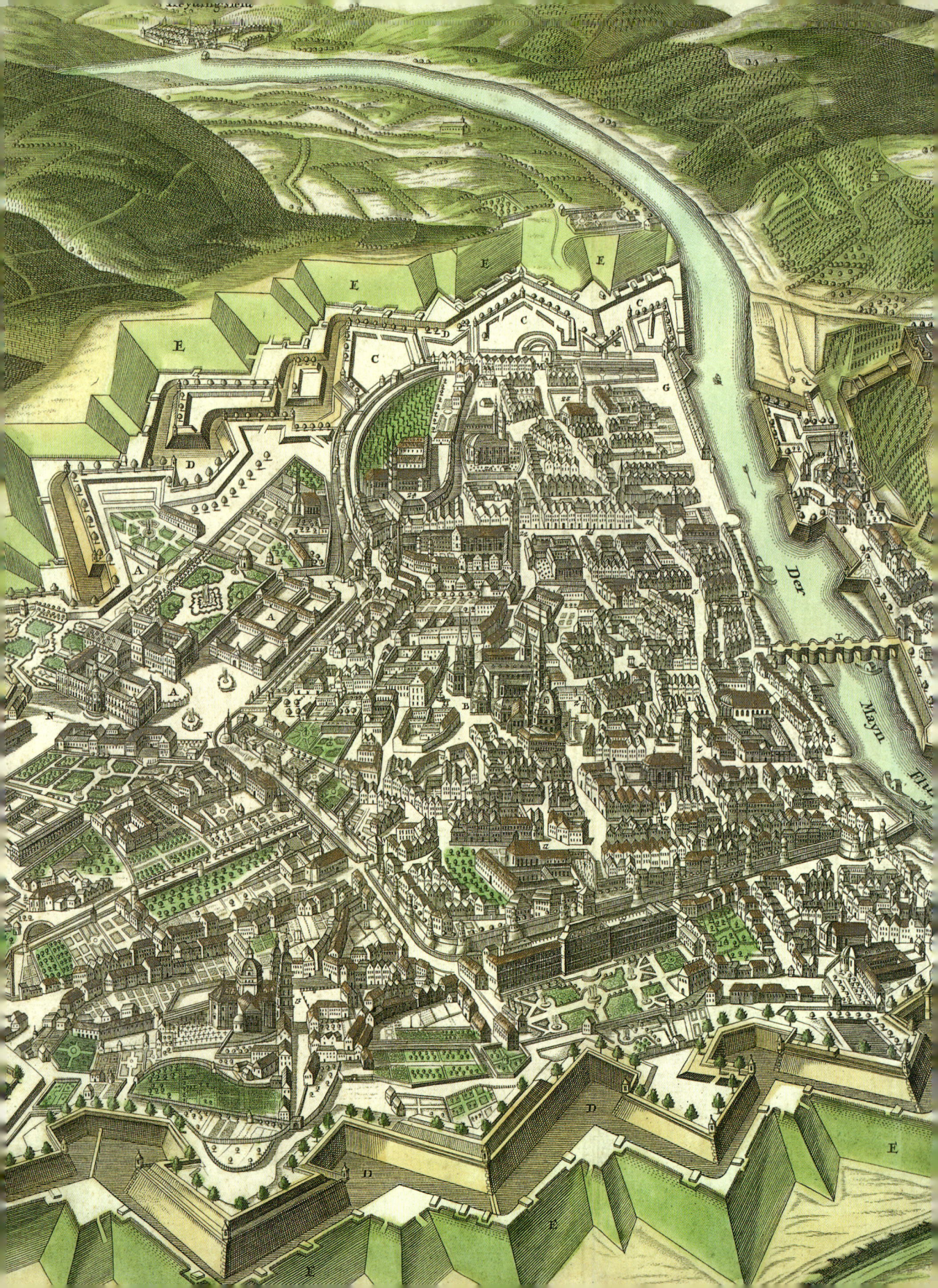

Der

Mayn
Fl:

28 *Monday*   Summer Bank Holiday, UK (exc. Scotland)

29 *Tuesday*

30 *Wednesday*

31 *Thursday*   *First Quarter*

1 *Friday*

2 *Saturday*

3 *Sunday*   Father's Day, Australia and New Zealand

Würzburg, 1723, showing the massive fortifications that were thrown up around so many European cities in the war-torn seventeenth century; those around the Marienberg fortress south of the River Main still survive. Maps 28855 (4)

SEPTEMBER

4 *Monday*   Holiday, Canada (Labour Day) and USA (Labor Day)

5 *Tuesday*

6 *Wednesday*

7 *Thursday*   *Full Moon*

8 *Friday*

9 *Saturday*

10 *Sunday*

Alexandria, as surveyed by members of the Napoleonic expedition of 1798, showing the city's location on an arm of rock between the Mediterranean and Lake Mareotis; no ancient maps of the city survive. The lower view shows one of Cleopatra's Needles, which now stands by London's river. 1899.k.1 (74) and 10094.h.1

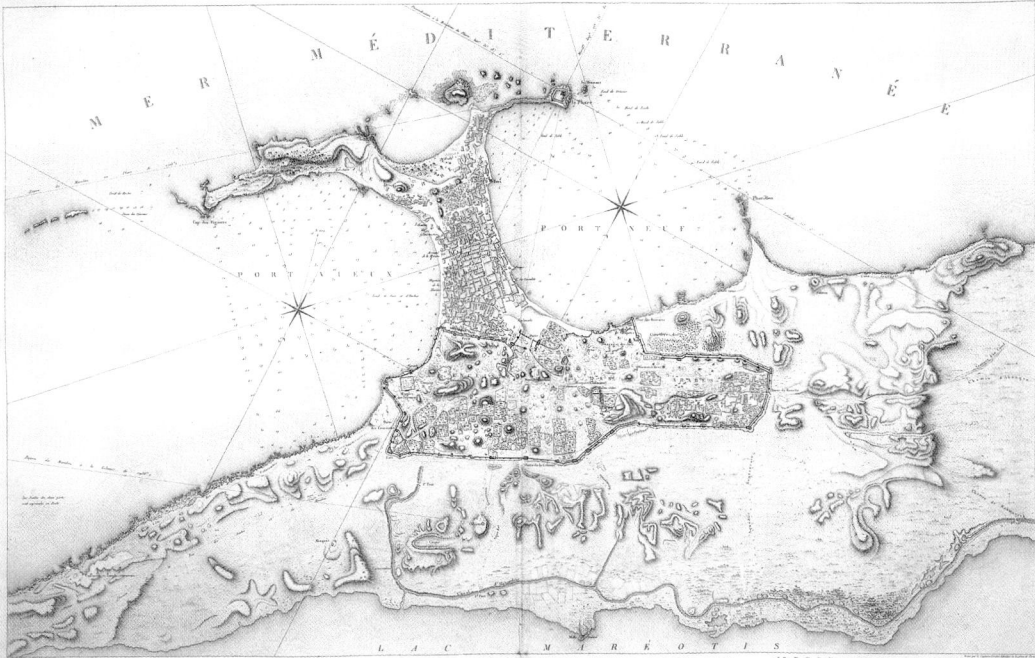

PLAN GÉNÉRAL DES DEUX PORTS, DE LA VILLE MODERNE, ET DE LA VILLE DES ARABES.

JAMSTERDAM

SEPTEMBER

11 *Monday*

12 *Tuesday*

13 *Wednesday*

14 *Thursday*   *Last Quarter*

15 *Friday*

16 *Saturday*

17 *Sunday*

Amsterdam in 1544, presided over by the sea god Neptune, source of the city's wealth. The view is from the north-east, with the original moorings on the Amstel in the centre. The city is beginning to spread to the west, beyond the Singel canal, where new canals will soon be dug. Maps STA (4)

SEPTEMBER

18 *Monday*

19 *Tuesday*

20 *Wednesday*

21 *Thursday*

22 *Friday* *New Moon*

23 *Saturday* Autumnal Equinox
Jewish New Year (Rosh Hashanah)

24 *Sunday* First Day of Ramadân (subject to sighting of the moon)

Isfahan, the Shah Mosque, a masterpiece of Persian blue tiling. N. Tab 2000/2

SEPTEMBER ✸ OCTOBER

25 *Monday*

26 *Tuesday*

27 *Wednesday*

28 *Thursday*

29 *Friday*   Michaelmas Day

30 *Saturday*   *First Quarter*

1   *Sunday*

Jerusalem, the most frequently imagined city in western art. Here it is depicted as a medieval European city, the crusaders camped outside its walls. Royal MS 1.E.IX, f.222

OCTOBER

2	*Monday*	Jewish Day of Atonement (Yom Kippur)

3 *Tuesday*

4 *Wednesday*

5 *Thursday*

6 *Friday*

7 *Saturday*

Jewish Festival of Tabernacles (Succoth), First Day
Full Moon

8 *Sunday*

St Andrews, the walls and churches of the ancient university town seen from the south in Slezar's *Theatrum Scotiae* of 1693. 188.f.2

COTHNISCHE Thor

Rondel Marckt

CÖPNICKSCHE

VORSTADT

Das Königl. Collegien Hauß

FRIEDRICHE VORSTADT

Jacobs Strasse
Koch Strasse
Zimmer Strasse
Schütz
Krau en Gasse
Leip Strasse

Francoische Capelle

Linden Marckt

Cronen Strasse

Molin von Strasse

Mittel Strasse

Jäger Strasse

Wilhelms Marckt

Cöpnicksche Strasse

C

B

P

Das Grosse Friedrichs Hospital

SPREE

D

Das Post Hauß

Königlicher Holtzmarckt

STRALAUER VORSTADT

Mühlen Strasse

Quer Strasse

Grüne Weg

Das Königl. Medicin Colleg.
Das Bauer Hauß

A

Die Juden Synagoga

Margareth Philipps Palair

DOROTHEEN VORSTAD

Mittel Strasse

Dorotheen Strasse

Der Kamecke sche Garten

Weiden damm

Damm

B. CÖLN.
Vier Theilen.
Spandauer Thor
Königs Thor
Stralauer Thor
Brücke nach Neu Cölln
Rasstrassen Brücke
Grünstrasse Br.
Gertrauden Brücke
Schleusen Br.
Münden Br.
Pomeranzen Br.
Burg Br.
Steinerne Br.
Mühlen Damm

KÖNIGS VORSTADT

Landsbergsche Strasse

Juden Abzug

Oranienburger Strasse
Juden begräb nüs

SPANDAUER VORSTADT

Mulack Gasse

Linden Marckt

Oranien Thor

Oranienburger

Rosenthaler Thor

Linien Strasse

Rosenthaler Thor

Das Zeug Hauß
Orange Hauß Die Garni son Kirch
Das Residentz Schloß
S. Marien Kirch
Die Dohm Kirch
S. Nicolai Kirch
Das Berlinsche Rath Hauß
S. Peters Kirch
Reformierte Pfarr Kirch
Kloster Kirch
S. Gertruden Spital in Cölln
Das Waijsen Hauß
Das Stralauische Thor
Das Cöpnicker Thor
Das Leipziger Thor
Das neue Thor

OCTOBER

9 *Monday*

Holiday, Canada (Thanksgiving Day)
Holiday, USA (Columbus Day)

10 *Tuesday*

11 *Wednesday*

12 *Thursday*

13 *Friday*

14 *Saturday*

Jewish Festival of Tabernacles (Succoth), Eighth Day
Last Quarter

15 *Sunday*

Berlin c.1730 by Seutter. The inner city is surrounded by canals dug from the River Spee and by massive walls, creating a fortress-like impression, around which suburbs are already developing. Maps 29720 (2)

OCTOBER

16 *Monday*

17 *Tuesday*

18 *Wednesday*

19 *Thursday*

20 *Friday*

21 *Saturday*

22 *Sunday*   *New Moon*

Calais, a dramatic view of the battle of 1558, in which France seized back England's last possession in Europe, occupied for over two centuries. The old town appears as a fortified island, set well back from the harbour. Maps C.7.c.4 (13)

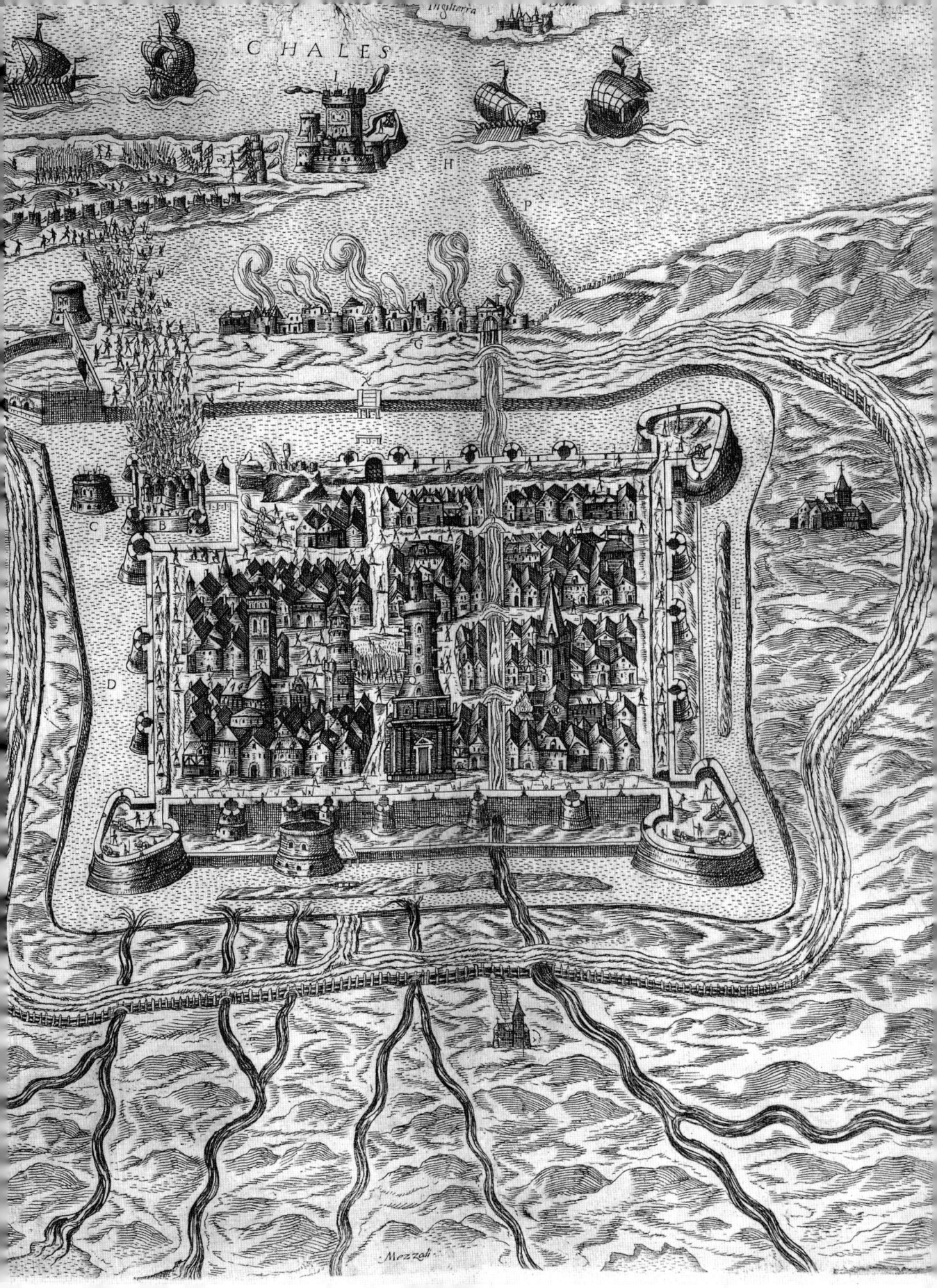

CHALES

BYZANTIVM NONC CONSTANTINOPOLIS

Palazo di Constantino Imperatore

Porta Constantina

Alma ratro

Patriarcato

Por chin

Theatro

S. Andrea

Tempis

Colose de spi riti

Colona storata

S. Pietro

Casa de pescatori

Voro

Porta de la farina

S. Constanti

S. Sebastiano

Colmna storata

Colona Serpentina

S. Tomas

Porta de le Pescari

Loco doue si paga li
montantia in ver Bor.

S. Sofia

Serraglio Nouo doue ha
bita el gran Turcho

Tennu

Palatio Com.

Pietra di calmstanu

Piaza

S. Maria Euanselita

Porta liona de
la Ruia

Porte
isole

chiamate principe
al sono habitate da
turchi

OCTOBER

23 *Monday*   Holiday, New Zealand (Labour Day)

24 *Tuesday*   United Nations Day

25 *Wednesday*

26 *Thursday*

27 *Friday*

28 *Saturday*

29 *Sunday*   British Summertime ends
First Quarter

Constantinople, by Braun and Hogenberg, 1572. This is now the Turkish city, with the Sultan's palace dominant in the foreground, and mosques replacing the churches. Maps C.29.e.1 (51)

30 *Monday*

31 *Tuesday* Hallowe'en

1 *Wednesday* All Saints' Day

2 *Thursday*

3 *Friday*

4 *Saturday*

5 *Sunday* Guy Fawkes' Day
Full Moon

Moscow, the Stone Bridge, also known as All Saints Bridge, built over the Moscow River in the seventeenth century, in a watercolour of 1801. LB.31.c.7277

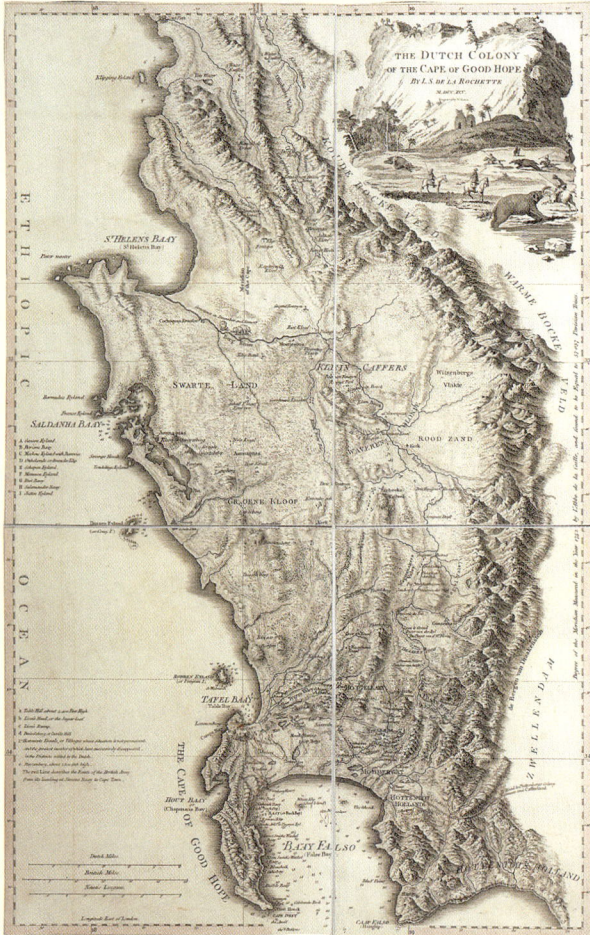

THE DUTCH COLONY
of the CAPE of GOOD HOPE
By L.S. DE LA ROCHETTE
MDCCXCV.

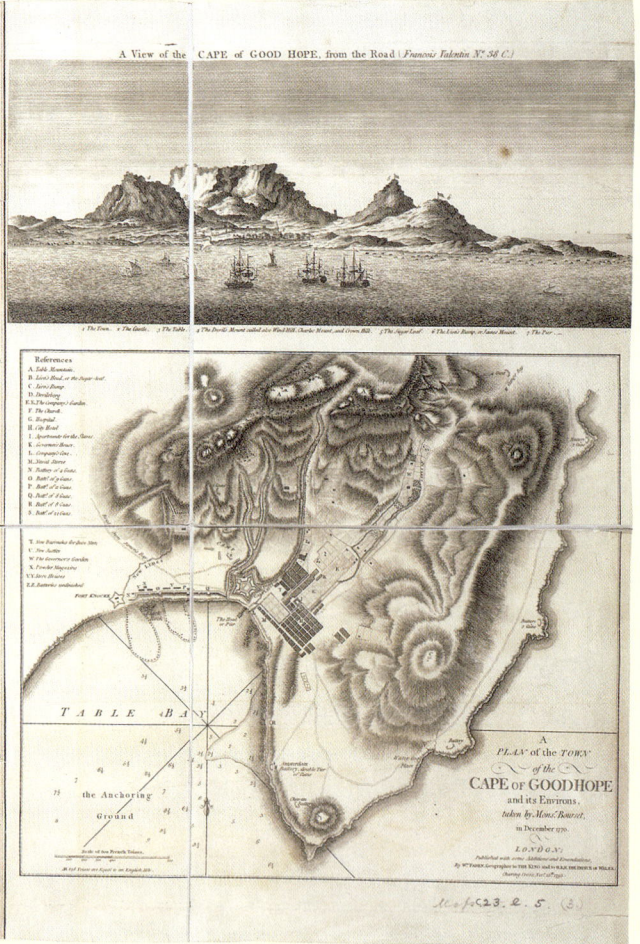

A View of the CAPE of GOOD HOPE, from the Road [Francois Valentin N.° 56 C.]

References

A PLAN of the TOWN
of the
CAPE of GOOD HOPE
and its Environs,
taken by Mons.r Bourat,
in December 1770.

LONDON;
Published with some Additions and Emendations,
By W.m FADEN Geographer to THE KING and to H.R.H. THE PRINCE of WALES,
Charing Cross, For L.S. Faget.

A
Draught of Cape
BONA ESPERANÇA
By Iohn Seller
Hydrographer to the
King

Charles's mount or
Crown Hill

Table

Sugar loaf

Iames Mount or
Lyons Rump

NOVEMBER

6 *Monday*

7 *Tuesday*

8 *Wednesday*

9 *Thursday*

10 *Friday*

11 *Saturday*   Holiday, Canada (Remembrance Day) and USA (Veterans' Day)

12 *Sunday*   Remembrance Sunday, UK
Last Quarter

Cape Town, a map of 1795 when the colony was still a Dutch possession, showing the tiny settlement against its rugged mountain hinterland. The lower view shows Table Mountain from the sea. Maps C.23.e.5 (3) and Maps C.8.b.13 (25)

NOVEMBER

13 *Monday*

14 *Tuesday*

15 *Wednesday*

16 *Thursday*

17 *Friday*

18 *Saturday*

19 *Sunday*

Stockholm, 1768, an engraved view of the waterfront at the city's heart. Maps K.Top. CXI.107a

NOVEMBER

20 *Monday*   *New Moon*

21 *Tuesday*

22 *Wednesday*

23 *Thursday*

24 *Friday*   Holiday, USA (Thanksgiving Day)

25 *Saturday*

26 *Sunday*

Lhasa c.1860, an anonymous Tibetan painting showing the Potala Palace and the Jokhang Temple from the south. Add. Or 3013

27 *Monday*

---

28 *Tuesday* *First Quarter*

---

29 *Wednesday*

---

30 *Thursday* St Andrew's Day

---

1 *Friday*

---

2 *Saturday*

---

3 *Sunday* Advent Sunday

Cologne, part of a panorama of 1500, with ships moored on the Rhine and the great cathedral under construction in the background. Maps 149.e.28 (2)

TEMPLV S. PETRI ET
S. TRIVM REGVM

S. GEREON

AD PREDICATORES

SENT LVPVS

FRANCKĒ TORN

AD MARIE GRADVS

T. MAXIMIN

die ney gros poert

RUINÆ EVERSÆ OLYSIPPONIS.   Ruin der Stadt Lisabona.

Portus major.

DECEMBER

4 *Monday*

5 *Tuesday*   *Full Moon*

6 *Wednesday*

7 *Thursday*

8 *Friday*

9 *Saturday*

10 *Sunday*

Lisbon, a dual view published in 1756 showing the old city above, and below the moment of the great earthquake of the previous year, with buildings collapsing into flaming ruins. Maps 11.e.2 (60)

DECEMBER

11 *Monday*

12 *Tuesday* *Last Quarter*

13 *Wednesday*

14 *Thursday*

15 *Friday*

16 *Saturday* Jewish Festival of Chanukah, First Day

17 *Sunday*

Liverpool, a plan of 1765, showing the old dock in the heart of the city, and an idyllic view of craft entering and leaving the pre-industrial port. Maps K.Top. XVIII 71 and Maps K.Top. XVIII 76c

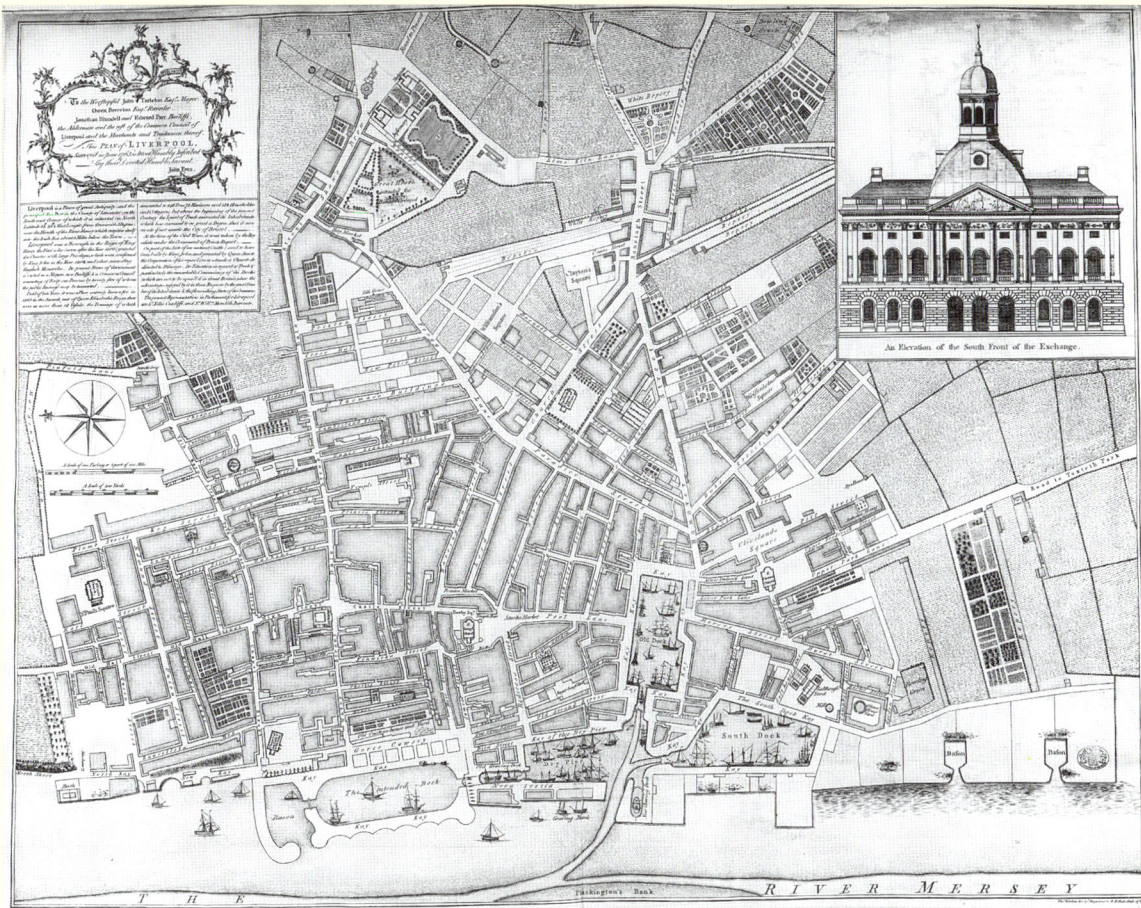

An Elevation of the South Front of the Exchange.

DECEMBER

18 *Monday*

19 *Tuesday*

20 *Wednesday*   *New Moon*

21 *Thursday*

22 *Friday*   Winter Solstice

23 *Saturday*

24 *Sunday*   Christmas Eve

Jerusalem, 1623. Like many views of the Holy City, different historical eras have been merged here, so that contemporary mosques are shown alongside Christian sites, real and imagined, and Solomon's Temple. Maps C.29.e.1 (2)

DECEMBER

25 *Monday*

Christmas Day
Holiday, UK, Republic of Ireland,
Canada, USA, Australia and New Zealand

26 *Tuesday*

Boxing Day (St Stephen's Day)
Holiday, UK, Republic of Ireland,
Canada, Australia and New Zealand

27 *Wednesday*

First Quarter

28 *Thursday*

29 *Friday*

30 *Saturday*

31 *Sunday*

New Year's Eve

Tangier c.1675 by John Seller. Tangier became a British possession in 1662. It was fortified and a great harbour was built, but frequent attacks by Moorish tribesmen made the town insecure, and it was evacuated in 1684.
Maps 7. Tab.77 (19)

Irish Battery

Port-Catharine

Governours house

Armes house

Stayners battery

The Upper Castle

NOTES

S. Dunsion inde vall

S. Michaels

S. Peter

Lambart hall

Lombar...

S. Mary Oueris

arke...